The definition of 'Magic Spanner'

MAGIC: The power to influence events via mysterious forces.

SPANNER: A tool for gripping or turning.

MAGIC SPANNER: The action of a mechanic to influence the recovery pace of a rider by way of mimicking a mechanical assist. Completed while hanging from a moving vehicle – thereby propelling the cyclist, at pace via automotive assistance, to regain time lost due to a racing incident.

MAGIC SPANNER

CARLTON KIRBY

WITH ROBBIE BROUGHTON

BLOOMSBURY SPORT
Bloomsbury Publishing Plc
50 Bedford Square, London, WC1B 3DP, UK

BLOOMSBURY, BLOOMSBURY SPORT and the Diana logo are trademarks of
Bloomsbury Publishing Plc

First published in Great Britain 2019

A catalogue record for this book is available from the British Library

Library of Congress Cataloguing-in-Publication data has been applied for

ISBN: TPB: 978-1-4729-5986-7; eBook: 978-1-4729-5985-0

2 4 6 8 10 9 7 5 3 1

Text design by seagulls.net

Typeset in Adobe Garamond Pro by Deanta Global Publishing Services, Chennai, India
Printed and bound in Great Britain by CPI Group (UK) Ltd. Croydon, CR0 4YY

To find out more about our authors and books visit www.bloomsbury.com
and sign up for our newsletters

CONTENTS

CONTENTS

FOREWORD BY SEAN KELLY

I reckon I've spent more July days in the company of Carlton than I have with anybody else these last few years. And I can tell you, he can be a challenge. As you all know he has a habit of going on a bit during commentary, and not just about the cycling. He can talk about anything . . . wherever he goes there are donkeys missing their hind legs. HE DOESN'T STOP! At the end of the day's action we get in the car and his mouth keeps racing. Thank heavens for Radio Monte Carlo and my control of the volume button; it's a useful tool.

I have been through my fair share of lead commentators and all have been very different. First there was David Duffield who started me off on the microphone. There was also Mike Smith, followed by David Harmon, and then Carlton Kirby along with Rob Hatch. They all have a different approach to their commentary; none sound the same. They have all been, or are, my teammates and I have enjoyed the company of them all both on and off air. It's fair to say we are privileged to have a job that generates so much fun around a sport we love.

Of course we have our moments but I've never come to blows with any of them; although I have thought about jamming a bread roll into Carlton's mouth a few times . . . he can go on . . . and on. He treats life as an adventure – a big one – and he certainly has a gift of bringing his anecdotes to life, as I'm sure you will find as you read on.

1
LIFE ON TOUR

4 a.m. A hotel in Paris. Day 20 of the Tour de France.

So there I am, dead of the night, a tubby middle-aged cycling nut locked out of his room . . . completely bollock naked. I'm waiting for the hotel security guy to let me back into my sanctuary. Considering my predicament, I'm remarkably at peace. Like a condemned man, I'm resigned to my situation. Bizarrely, I'm pondering what to do with my arms. There are no pockets to look nonchalant; folded arms would look a bit showy-offy. Inevitably, as there is little to be proud of, two hands are cupped over my man bits. I wait, breaking my serenity only occasionally to whisper 'Aaaaw, shut up' to the Japanese tourists trapped in the escape stairwell in front of me. For it is they who got me into this mess. They are getting restive. . . Well, they'll have to wait.

The best part of three weeks on the road have taken their toll: 6 a.m. starts, hours of driving, hours of staring at a small TV monitor while commentating on the greatest sporting event on earth. Le Hexagon as it's called – or 'France', to you and me – is a remarkable arena. And a big place. It takes a lot of getting around, which has left me shattered; physically exhausted, mentally frazzled. Still, though, I have just enough brain space to ponder a diversion: it's amazing how much temperature and surface definition you can sense via a buttock! Yep, my door felt cold and smooth to the touch . . . 'but I'm not using my hands. Amazing.'

My predicament started with a gently strumming sound that entered my dreams. Darrrum, darrrum, darrrum . . . *What the hell is that?* I asked myself. Darrrum, darrrum, darrrum . . . Like a kid drumming four fingers on a table, impersonating a horse. Or a classic Hollywood scene of someone losing patience. Darrrum, darrrum, darrrum, darrrum. It went on. At my bloody door! 'SHAAAADAAAAP!' I shouted. And it stopped. Then, just as I'm nodding back off, there it was again. This time I hurled a fine Crockett and Jones bootie at the door and screamed: '*F------k offf!*' for good measure. The effect was the same. A brief halt before the strumming was back again.

For me, there is a Rule of Three when it comes to being woken up. My wife is familiar with this. Once is okay. Twice may be forgivable. Third time? All done. I'm up and out of bed. Grumpy as they come, usually flamboyantly knotting a dressing gown as I head for the kitchen and a cuppa. This was far more serious. I was deeply fatigued and in no mood to reason. I was going to tell these bastards just what I thought of them, my dark mood accentuated by the entirety of my blue-white nakedness. Furious, I yanked the door open with a backed-up series of expletives about to let rip.

There was absolutely nobody there!

The corridor was completely empty save for the rolled-up fire hose next to my room at the end of a long blank corridor with mood lighting and an awful Aztec-print carpet. Silence.

Then just as I'm convincing myself I am clearly going mad . . . it started again. The sound was coming from behind the fire doors directly opposite mine. 'Bastards!' I thought. Kids just pissing about. Well here we go then, have some of this!

It was about now that my world went into slow motion. Holding my door handle, I pivoted Sumo style and launched a kick directly at the Push Bars To Open sign, the idea being that the miscreants would be sent flying as the doors flew open into the stairwell.

Wham! The doors smashed open against the concrete walls.

Now, screaming is an auto-reaction, usually in response to the perception of exaggerated threat. On this occasion the threat levels were considered high on both sides of the fire doors' threshold.

The screams from both directions went on for a few elongated seconds. The Japanese tourists rocked back en masse at the sight of a Sumo/Bjarne Riis lookalike. Meanwhile, I simply lost control of the situation. Still screaming, I grabbed both bars and slammed the fire doors back shut.

Clunk! went the fire doors. Then, *Clunk* went the door of my room.

Bent over and still holding the bars of the fire doors, I looked over my shoulder, knowing I was in trouble. 'Aaaaaaaw, for God's sake!'

Next to the hose was a red telephone. I picked it up. There was no need to dial. It began ringing at the front desk. Security answered.

'Oui!'

'Bonsoir, Monsieur. C'est Monsieur Kirby. J'ai un petit predicament! Um . . . I'm locked out of my room.'

'OK, I'll come up and let you in.'

'Um, I must warn you that I'm actually, um, en nue . . . naked. Completely. And. . .'

'Yes?'

'There are some Japanese tourists locked in the stairwell.'

Just as he puts the phone down, I hear him start to laugh.

Darrrum, darrrum, darrrum . . .

'All right, I know you're there . . . give it a bleedin' rest.'

What seems like an age goes by before: *POING!* Finally the lift announces its arrival.

I prepare to greet the security guard. But it's not the security guard.

It was an elderly American couple who must have enjoyed the same night out at the Moulin Rouge as my Japanese friends. Unlike my pals in the stairwell, they had seen the sign for the Night Porter's bell. The Japanese guests had thought they were locked out and duly made their way up the fire escape in the hope of waking some kindly soul who would let them in. Well, it didn't go too well for them, did it? Likewise my American friends.

'Good evening,' I ventured.

'Oh. My. God!' said the lady.

Terror begets clumsiness. The air was now filled with the sound of the frantic swiping of the door key as the theatregoers desperately tried to gain entry. It opened and they crashed through their door, slamming it behind them. I could hear her crying.

POING! At last the security guard comes strolling down the corridor. He's smiling and biting a lip while politely half-covering his eyes. 'Good evening, Monsieur Kirby,' he ventures as his linked phone goes off. It's the Americans.

'Yes, Security?' he answers. 'A naked man in the corridor. Yes sir, I'm dealing with that now.'

I slip, albeit slightly camply, into my room.

'Merci, Alphonse! Don't forget the Japanese.'

Welcome to *Magic Spanner: The World of Cycling according to Carlton Kirby*. Join me on a journey into both the heart and the margins of the world's greatest sport, where we ponder a Universal Truth: every time something goes right, something must also go wrong. So, let's get on and expose the rather odd bits that have accompanied me and this crazy sport! Enjoy.

'HE'S SCREAMING . . . ALBEIT SILENTLY.'

2
THE BREAKFAST OF KINGS

The Cast

Sean Kelly: aka The King, seven times consecutive winner of Paris–Nice, among other marvels. Now a commentator for Eurosport.

Greg LeMond: Three-time winner of the Tour de France and former World Champion. Consultant to Eurosport.

Kathy LeMond: Greg's wife, informal manager and bodyguard.

Pascal: Greg's fixer – and litter bin kicker, given to theatrical displays of displeasure – who makes sure everything's in order for his boss.

Dan Lloyd: former British professional cyclist. Now a lead presenter for GCN and co-commentator for Eurosport.

And me, Carlton Kirby: TV commentator for Eurosport.

6 a.m. A hotel somewhere hot in Italy. The Giro is in full swing. I stumble down for breakfast after a night spent vibrating windows with my snoring,

to find Sean Kelly sitting behind a pile of mush. This is not unusual. You might think that King Kelly would be given to enjoying a choice bowl of muesli, a yogurt perhaps or maybe some fresh fruit. This would certainly have a better look about it – and such fare is being enjoyed by other cycling royals sitting not five paces to my left. Greg LeMond, the Duke of Des Moines, is in the building, which instantly proves two things: 1. There is air conditioning in this building (no air con, no Greggie boy); and 2. This is as upmarket as it gets in this particular location. This is LeMond Central and Greg is up in every sense. In fact, if Greg is awake, he's up! Up for anything. This human being has an on switch like no other. Full on. I love him. Greg is partying – at breakfast. Loud and lovely with his amazing wife, Kathy, and his pocket enforcer, Pascal, who is exceptional in many ways: he's everywhere, he knows everybody, is super-friendly and speaks numerous languages, all with a heavy French accent. He's a tiny guy who makes up for his diminutive height by sticking his arms out to make himself look bigger, hands on hips. You could actually put him in your pocket, though.

So cycling royalty are tucking in. As loud and welcoming as the LeMond corner is, I head for the pile of mush. 'Morning, Sean.' To which the long-drawn-out response is always: 'Alright', in his southern Irish lilt.

So we have got the conversation ball rolling. To be fair, there is not much further for it to go before we get on air. 'Sleep well, Sean?' . . . pause . . . 'Not bad. Me back's a bit—' (grimaces). And that's it.

So what is Kelly eating? Baguette husks with hard cheese and regular jam as well. The food of champions. Or it was for many years. This is Belgian bikers' brekkie. 'Too many bloody carbs in the middle bit,' Sean once explained. So, like many old-school riders have done for decades, he pulls out the soft centre of every baguette, then fills the empty shell with cheese and jam. Yum.

The mantra goes on. Not content with pulling out the fluffy bit, Sean moulds it into what I am sure were once the missiles of his youth. Not that he's throwing them any more – he simply plays with them until they turn grey and have the texture of Blu-Tack.

'Righty-oh. Eight thirty OK?'

'Yep, see you then.' And with that he's gone.

'Carol Tone! Come and join us!' It takes me a second to realise Kathy, as warm as ever, is talking to me and has kept me a place.

As I slide in, Greg launches:

'Eggs! There's gotta be a better way! Eggs are different sizes, right? Water boils at different temperatures depending on altitude, right? So there is no genuine rule that says an egg is guaranteed soft boiled in three minutes, right? You know I'm right. So here's the thing, we develop an egg sensor. I dunno, x-rays, ultrasound, there's gotta be a way. A better way. Whaddya think, Crayol Tun?'

'Greg, I don't really mind how my eggs turn out.'

'Well, I care!' says Greg. 'Look at all these, for cryin' out loud. None of 'em right.'

In front of him Greg has probably eight eggs, all open and uneaten. None have passed the newly coined Greg's Eggs Test. It's about now I'm reminded of the teacher in *Charlie Brown* whose voice is a background muffle. 'Mumble mumble eggs mumble mumble. Technology mumble mumble.'

'You OK, Kathy?' She goes from dazed to electrified in a second.

'Sure am! Never better. How's it going? How's Sean's driving holding up?'

Kathy is a marvel. I love chatting to her. I'm just about to go into Sean's latest mountain rally session when *bam!* I'm slapped on the shoulder by Greg:

'Ultraviolet! Doesn't the wavelength alter depending on surface resistance? Does this change with the solidifying of the egg's core?'

'I don't know, Greg.'

Dan Lloyd, anchor for Global Cycling Network (GCN) and an ex-pro, walks in. He's wearing sunglasses he bought for too much money in a junk shop on the Adriatic coast. Green plastic Gucci, with graded brown lenses from the 1980s. On me they'd look dreadful. On Dan they're just right. Certainly right for his hangover.

Two things get Dan animated: beer and money. He hates spilling either: 'You owe me €60.'

'What?'

Dan takes a weary sigh. Like a teenager faced with a parent he has lost all respect for, he takes a long breath and then fires off a staccato series of thoughts, all nailed together as a sentence, designed to fend off any interruption or any form of argument.

'We got towed last night, you told me to park over by the garage, it's the finish line, they lifted us last night, it's €120, so you owe me €60.'

Without waiting for any reply he stands up, downs a cappuccino in one and leaves the breakfast room without another word.

It's time to go.

'IT'S A BIT OF A DOG'S BREAKFAST. OTHER BREAKFASTS ARE AVAILABLE.'

3
DRIVE TO THE FINISH

7 a.m. The morning drive to the TV enclosure isn't usually too bad, as we'll have arrived in the middle of the night close to where we're supposed to be. It gives us a chance to take a good look at what the finish will be like for the riders, and we'll make various notes about what the pinch points are likely to be, where a rider can attack and what they'll need to watch out for. Normally, Sean will be driving at this point, so I'll be there, pen and paper in hand, as he makes lots of technical comments and/or expletives like: 'Feck. That's going to be shit!'

Sean is a master at finding a parking spot. This is absolutely vital to ensure a speedy getaway at the end of the day. Naturally, it helps being a former Grand Tour winner, and police and security guards seem to be queuing up to help him out. In France, he's a huge name: everyone still remembers his seven consecutive victories in Paris–Nice and his string of stage wins on the Tour, Giro and his Vuelta title, not to mention his victories in the Monuments (classics) including Paris–Roubaix and Milan–San Remo.

This means he's given a bit more leeway than others who might get flagged to one side. Even so, finding the right spot to leave the car still remains something of an art. Occasionally even Sean gets this wrong, like when he parked in the pitch of an ice cream seller, who decided to block us in for revenge. Or the time we were given the thumbs up by a local cop who had his parking ticket book signed by Sean. All was good until we got the call from Captain Black – or the Tour de France Head of Facilities, to give him his official title. Upset him, and you're off the race. And I mean *off*. Sean had to leave the commentary position while we were on air to move his car – or else. Seemed he'd parked in the Team Cannondale coach bay and had precisely two minutes to move it. Well, our position was about two miles away. Sean got there – and again found out how lucky he is to be him. The car was lifted back off the low loader, probably in acknowledgement of his Paris–Nice record. He also kept his all-important press badges.

One commentator – Italian, I believe – suffered the ultimate sanction in such a situation: The Badge Rip! It's a bit like the flamboyant stripping of all medals and stripes from a tunic before your execution by firing squad: your passes are yanked from your neck. At least there's a breaker clip just above the badges to prevent you suffering a neck injury. Our Italian friend suffered this fate and was relegated to describing the Tour from the TV in his hotel room despite the inevitable delay between the action and his voice. His commentary was about 10 seconds late throughout. Not good in a sprint finish. He was replaced two days later.

For me, if I'm not with Sean, parking is a nightmare because no one is willing to help and I don't have 'the gift', as my friend calls it. And if we happen to be in a medieval hilltop village, the roads and gradients are difficult to negotiate. If there's one smell that defines the Tour de France for me, it's the acrid reek of a burning clutch as underpowered hire cars are forced up gradients of 20%. But Sean has an amazing knack of finding little side streets where we're not too far away but can still make a speedy escape ahead of the huge caravan that is the Tour de France. Sometimes he'll drop me off while he parks up and will come up to me later, immensely proud of the prime spot he's found. 'I've found a great place. Fantastic place. We'll be out of here in no time.' And he's usually right.

'THIS CLIMB IS LIKE A SLAP IN THE FACE WITH A WET KIPPER.'

THE PUBLICITY CARAVAN

You're new to the game. You've graduated from clown work entertaining kids at the burger bar and now you've landed the big one: your pass says Publicity Caravan, and that gives you a special place in the race. You will be first along the day's route, first to get away once the course clears of riders – and the last to arrive at your destination. Why? Because you are to drive one of the most unwieldy vehicles ever allowed on to public roads.

You have just been handed the keys to an open-topped VW Beetle that has been transformed, by a skilled fabricator, into what now resembles powered castors beneath a plastic log cabin 6m (20ft) high, from which a honey bear 3m (10ft) tall is leaning out of a window giving his famous (in France) winky, grinny, thumbs-up salute. Something he has been doing since a so-called design guru dropped the 72-year-old bee logo of this famous honey brand in favour of this 'Awesome Orson' back in 1983. It's now your job to drive this monstrosity on an extremely hazardous three-week journey all over France, while battling wind and rain, mountain roads and country lanes, motorways and city centres. Progress will be slow. *Very* slow. However, despite journeys that are sometimes six hours long, you *will* smile *all the time*. It's in the contract.

Welcome to the world of Grand Tour Publicity, the commercial circus that pays the bills and causes grown men and old ladies alike to fight small children in order to grab the most modest of freebies hurled from some of the very odd-looking vehicles that pass by the massed ranks of cycling fans and confused tourists at the roadside on each stage of every day of the tour.

Every Grand Tour has a publicity caravan. These are the engine room of the sponsors' summertime promotional push to the masses that gather, sometimes 20 deep, along the roadside of the biggest annual open-access sporting events on the planet. The public loves the publicity caravan. Those working on the race, not so much. And if you feel sorry for those driving these glass-fibre behemoths, then spare a thought for those of us stuck behind the damn things. They are a bloody nuisance, particularly when trying to get around them on a mountain pass. I hate Awesome Orson and his brothers in plastic arms.

Due to safety reasons, the publicity caravan makes rather modest progress along the road. These unwieldy floats are regarded as dangerous at more than 65km/h (40mph). So, in deference to the poor sods who have to drive them for near inhuman lengths of time, there is a vogue among race organisers to let the caravan set off ahead of the press corps at the end of each day's stage. This is not appreciated by those wishing to get in some solid wine time after a hard day's broadcasting. So whine time it is, then; particularly if we happen to be going up a mountain road, where overtaking opportunities are few and far between.

Many risks have been taken as Kelly goes for it on a slightly straight bit of road, only to be faced by an oncoming car that means we have to force our way into a modest gap between the Haribo Kid and a giant leg of ham. Having been forced to back off, the driver of the leg of ham now goes for the familiar salute – a blast from the horn – only to realise he's forgotten that it's been rewired, and now fires a plinkety-plonkety theme tune, accompanied by a song blaring from those 'The circus is coming to town' speakers:

Jam-bon, jam-bon, s'il vous plaît, Ma-man,
Ma-man, Ma-man, s'il vous plaît jam-bon.

All this while showing us the internationally recognised sign 'You're Number 1'... well, it was just the one finger; I'm sure that's what he meant. Though he wasn't smiling.

One of the saddest sights I think I've ever seen was a clearly demotivated teenager in a thick velour banana outfit staring forlornly at the ground as his 'boss', no more than a couple of years older, was busy giving him a pep talk before he began his gig at the finish line: 'Alfonse, you have to feel it! You have to want it! That's your public out there . . . and we are going to give them what they want. That's you and your gifts! *Come on*, they will love you. So let's *feel* the love. Take control of the moment. Throw those banana candies high and proud! *Feed* them! *Honour* them! OK?'

Alfonse said nothing. It was 36°C (97°F) and he was clearly suffering. An hour later, I noticed a big yellow banana was being stretchered off course. Heatstroke, I believe.

'IT'S DÉJÀ VU ALL OVER AGAIN.'

4
SECURITY, GOOD AND BAD

10 a.m. The Tour de France TV compound, Bergerac, France.

It's around two hours before we go on air. We have arrived and parked the car in what Sean Kelly describes as 'A prime bit o' real estate'. This means we will get away quickly later. I retrieve my bag from the back of the car without disturbing Sean's underwear, which he has hung up to dry in the day's heat. People always wonder why our car is usually steamed up. I saunter up to a man who looks like he could have arrived by parachute. He is dressed in near fatigues and wired for sound and armed with several devices of varying degrees of lethality. He is demonstrably well conditioned and looks like his spit may contain nails.

Me: 'Bonjour, Monsieur, est-ce la zone de presse ici?'

CRS officer: Silence

Me, again: 'S'il vous plaît monsieur, est qu'il—'

CRS officer: 'Allez!'

This conversation was now over. It was also probably the best outcome you can get when interacting with a member of France's riot police, the CRS. Simply being told to go away was a bonus. Communication is apparently something these guys reserve only for themselves. They live in compounds with well-equipped gymnasia and shooting ranges. They are a breed apart. Welcome to the fittest and meanest division in the hierarchy of the French police.

At the bottom of the pecking order of Les Flics, you find your local police; often chubby and driving tatty Renault Clios. Like all police here, they are armed, but in their case their weapons probably get drawn only for compulsory practice.

As you rise up the pecking order, you go through the regional police, with slightly better cars as well as slightly better levels of intellect and fitness. Go higher and higher, and you will get to the Presidential Guard. Basically the equivalent of the SAS. Close to this pinnacle is a subdivision marked 'Hard' where you find a utility division called the CRS, Les Compagnies Républicaines de Sécurité, but otherwise known as Car Rempli des Singes (cart-load of monkeys). This is the Riot Squad.

As you may have gathered, they are not necessarily here to serve the public: they are here to control the public. The clue's in the name; their job is to police riots. And that means no small talk or indeed any talk at all – unless they are letting their fists do it. 'Don't mess with the CRS', says the T-shirt.

By and large, most people attached to the Tour de France are glad to have the CRS in the vicinity. Those who ignore them are in more trouble than they realise. Indeed, this trouble can come rather quickly and, be warned: you will bruise. The regular police can, to a certain degree, be messed with. You can ask a regular cop, 'Why?' and he may take the time to wearily explain his instructions. But with the CRS, you get just one chance. I took the order 'Allez!' with good grace and did indeed *allez* rather quickly. Others have, in the past, fared less well. The CRS can get a little, well, enthusiastic. Like with Antler Man, for instance.

Antler Man was a crazy American cycling fan who'd turn up on the Grand Tours wearing an American Football style helmet, sometimes with bison horns, ram horns or moose antlers attached to it. Known variously as the Raging Stag, Moose Man and Antler Man, his real name was Dore Holt and he was an aircraft mechanic from Seattle. He'd run ahead of the riders waving the Stars and Stripes with this ridiculous headgear on and he made a nuisance of himself because he couldn't go as fast as the riders, even uphill. As he looked round, he'd come close to knocking off the riders with the horns sticking out of his helmet.

My fellow Eurosport commentator Juan Antonio Flecha, who used to ride for Sky, told me of when he once snatched Antler Man's flag off him in the middle of a race because the American was annoying him so much. He then rode with it for a hundred metres or so before chucking it to the side of the road. Later on in the day he saw him and apologised for taking the flag.

'I don't mind you taking the flag,' Dore Holt said. 'But you didn't respect the flag. You threw the flag away.'

Antler Man was a royal pain in the arse and I always made a point of ridiculing him in my commentary, so I hope I had something to do with his recent absence from major races. He was warned many times by the police, but he just wouldn't keep away and continued appearing on mountain stages, getting in the way and coming close to poking various eyes out with his antlers – the eyes of riders, of spectators, and of the CRS.

When the CRS have had enough of such miscreants, they often decide to throw them into the back of the van. Sometimes before they've remembered to open the doors. It's a statement.

We haven't seen much of Antler Man in Europe in recent years, although I understand he still likes to ply his trade back in the US.

'HE WAS ON THE LINE BUT IT WAS FULL OF WASHING.'

5
THE FIVE LIONS

While we are pondering the characters that surround the Grand Tours, it's probably worth taking a moment to talk of the guys at the top of the game. They're British, don't you know!

2018 was when the Three Lions of British cycling became Five. We had Cav, Wiggo and Froomie. And then Geraint Thomas produced a truly remarkable display of selfless dedication and opportunism to land the biggest prize in cycling. G went from super-domestique to King of the Hill in just 21 remarkable stages to win the Tour de France. Then La Vuelta beckoned. Simon Yates went for it, and became part of an historic record. I can't stop saying it: Three Grand Tours with three different riders all from the same nation!? Likely as not, this will never be repeated. In cycling terms, it's epic.

As we well know, we find ourselves in the middle of a now well-established cycling era. It's British, and our friends on the continent do not like this fact one little bit. Europeans began to wake up to the threat in the early 1990s. British track success was generating a little mild amusement at Eurosport's hub in Paris, where Patrick Chasse, the then doyen of all things cycling on the channel, would pontificate: 'Graeme Obree! With his washing machine bits and bobs. Formidable!'

It was, of course, damning with faint praise. This mild mockery took another turn with the arrival of Chris Boardman, who began to smash records all over the place on the track and time trial bike. Chasse again: 'He is a freaky one-off, on a spooky bike! Good luck to him.' But he wasn't a one-off, of course. This was the start of something very special in British cycling. There had been other greats in the past and, to be fair, why should continental cycling have feared a couple of Brits and their 'funny machines'? Nonetheless, just to make sure these interlopers didn't get above their station, rules were changed regarding machinery in the velodrome and on the courses. 'Bicycles must look like bicycles' was the UCI edict. If a bike did not fit to the strict parameters of what was defined as an acceptable competition bike, you could not ride it. The simple fact was that the geometry of the frame was to be the parameter. The new rules hobbled progress a little, but British success was no cheap firework display with a few pops and bangs in a remote car park. It was the start of a magnificent extravaganza, the like of which has not been seen in cycling. For a nation to come from the sidelines to become *the* reference point in terms of the entire approach to the sport was nothing short of seismic.

Cycling was a sport that many thought would always belong to the Old World on the European mainland: France, Belgium and Italy, with Spain carrying some bragging rights as well. That's the way it always was, and many of those nations wished it to be just so for ever. But change had come and now at the top of the hill, for the time being at least, sits Great Britain. For a time we were great at hitting and kicking balls of various shapes and sizes, and when we went racing it was with horses, boats or motors. But now we also happen to be very, very good at cycling. Something of a dynasty has been created.

The last 10 years have seen a phenomenal rise in the prominence of British riders. This has in turn generated a huge following for cycling in the UK.

TV audience figures have gone through the roof, particularly for the Grand Tours but also the Monuments (classics) and the great preparation races such as the Dauphiné or Tour de Romandie. As a result, participation has grown exponentially; people are getting on their bikes, huge numbers joining local clubs and taking part in sportives. The fan base is clearly visible at the roadside during races such as the Tour of Britain as well as the Tour de Yorkshire, newly elevated to a 2.HC event on the UCI Europe Tour. This after Yorkshire hosted the Grand Départ of the 2014 Tour de France with phenomenal success. Côte de Buttertubs may not have the resonance of Mont Ventoux or Alpe d'Huez, but it most certainly sits in a new crucible of great cycling venues.

The Cambridge Dictionary defines *crucible* as 'a place or situation in which different cultures or styles can mix together to produce something new and exciting'. That, my friends, is British cycling. Sorry, everybody else, it's true.

Over the years I've got to know our heroes to varying degrees. We are members of the same travelling circus, after all. I've seen them on and off air, before and after races, chatted, and even shared taxi rides. So I've been able to gain some insight into what makes them tick. Although I come from the position of a professional commentator, I am also a huge fan of all of them. I admire their achievements hugely and indeed often become highly emotional while calling the exploits and witnessing their triumphs as well as their failures.

Our heroes have found success in most of the varying forms of racing, dependent on their body shapes, motivation, skills and character traits. Our five Lions are all very different but have each in their own way contributed immeasurably to the spectacular success of British cycling.

MARK CAVENDISH

Interviewer: 'So, Mark, you have a problem: you have won a Harley Davidson! How are you going to split this with your HTC teammates?'

Cav [beginning to grin broadly]: 'Um.' [*Shrugs his shoulders.*] 'F--k 'em!'

Mark Cavendish is a fast man oddity; slight of frame yet a sprinting machine, whose reaction time, tactics and phenomenal aero position helped him become World Champion and winner of the points jersey in all three Grand Tours. He's obsessed with perfection and, as I write, he has 30 Tour de France stage victories to his name.

In 2003, when Mark came over from the Isle of Man to join British Cycling in Manchester, he was seen as a bit of an enigma. On the one hand he was winning races on the track, but when the statisticians looked at his numbers, his lung capacity, power outputs and so on didn't quite add up. The analysts said he fell short of what was required to be an elite rider. Put simply, at a height of 1.75m (5ft 9in), he was told he was not only too short but also too stocky to be a cyclist, especially if he was looking for a career on the road. Well, how wrong were they!

Thank the Lord that Mark Cavendish has bags of self-belief. Mark simply redoubled his determination to prove the numbers men wrong. He still talks about making them eat their words. It's an injustice that smoulders deep inside the man. He refers to it occasionally in a valedictory kind of way.

You see, Mark has proved that sprinting is not simply about power. He's rewritten the profile on what makes a great sprinter. So let's ponder why he is able to win so often with far more powerful guys around him.

Firstly: aerodynamics. This plays a huge part. Mark is able to hunch over his bike in the most amazing aerodynamic position – one that isn't matched by anybody other than the young Australian Caleb Ewan, who mirrors Cav by placing his chin almost touching the front wheel over the handlebars.

Physically, Mark is far smaller than most of the sprinters around him, so he naturally faces far less wind resistance than his bigger opponents. This advantage is compounded by the fact that if Mark follows the big guys he gets a bigger assist than when they follow his wheel.

Genetics also play a part. Tests have shown Cav to possess a fast twitch muscle response that is remarkably quick. This means the command from brain to body for action is exponentially quicker than that enjoyed by almost anybody else. His explosive response to a cerebral command is virtually unmatched.

Mix these significant advantages with remarkable brainpower, bike-handling and his very personality, and you have a winning combination that has made him the most successful sprinter of a generation, maybe of all time.

Usefully, Mark possesses a near photographic memory of every sprint finish he's ever done. Whether it's one from yesterday or 10 years ago, he will clinically dissect each one in such a way that he could write a chapter on every stage he's ever contested, whether it ended in victory or defeat.

That mental sharpness is something that he hones and develops through brain exercises and mental challenges. He's a demon Rubik's Cubist and uses what he calls a brain gym app to test and stretch himself. Clearly he likes his brain to be as fast as his legs. If he's won, he will tell you exactly how he did it, who was doing what, where they were, what they were thinking, what wheel he chose and the point at which he decided to make his move.

One example from 2017: 'Today was a bit like Missouri back in 2008, when Chicchi was making a nuisance of himself, Michael and Bernie did an amazing job: punched through and I just feathered it past Farrar's left; with about 60 to go and went for it.' If he's lost, he is likely not to tell you a thing, but it's all in there in his head and you can bet that he'll have a few choice words to say to his team at the dinner table.

In terms of bike-handling, there have been a few blips – some requiring surgery. But it's because he's seeing a percentage opportunity in any gap;

this has to be calculated in milliseconds. Most gaps he successfully masters. It's a function of his track background in the tight and hectic world of madison racing.

Now, it's all very well having the physical and mental capacity to be a world-class sprinter, but the delivery platform for these attributes is self-belief. You need to have it. And Mark does. Totally. As clinical and focused as a surgeon, he expects everyone else around him to race with the same level of investment. These are high standards. He sets them for himself. And woe betide anyone who falls short out there. Sprinting is a war zone and Mark is the field marshal.

It was when he was riding for HTC that he really developed into a world-class sprinter. Mark Renshaw, Bernie Eisel and André Greipel were the three generals who made a remarkable lead-out force that changed the way sprinting was approached. Their train was omnipotent, but the pressure to fall in behind Cav got too much for some and its phenomenal run eventually came to an end.

Years later, and by now on different teams, Greipel went on to beat Mark in a bunch sprint at the Tour de France. It was a strange, cathartic celebration as he crossed the line. All the years of pressure that had built while working for Cav bubbled up with a primal and tearful scream as he crossed the line. It seemed to me that, for Greipel, the confirmation that he'd had the talent to win all along was devastating rather than liberating.

High standards mean high pressure. Mark is generous with praise for his team if all goes well. They are the first to get a mention ahead of any analysis of his own effort. But he will also judge and castigate himself for any mistake or poor performance, and his team will be in the cross hairs of his mood – particularly any teammate he feels has fallen short.

I recall him being interviewed after a 'fail' and really having a go at Bernie Eisel for a poor lead out that went awry on the first stage of the Tour of Abu Dhabi in 2016. At the sign-in for the following day, under the gaze of the world's cycling press and spectators, Cav began walking off the stage. Without turning round even to look, he disdainfully proffered the pen over his shoulder to Eisel in what looked like a public display of contempt. This was Cav reminding his teammate that all was not forgiven for the previous day's mistakes. More was expected of him. Of course, Cav and the team then went on to win the day.

Cav can be notoriously difficult to interview if he's uncomfortable with any question that happens to be: 1. too probing; 2. disrespectful; or 3. plain stupid. He has torn journalists apart in the past. This, of course, can be most amusing to those witnessing. If he's getting stressed for any of the above reasons, he'll either go completely silent or fire an aggressive question back. The giveaway is an anger twitch in his jaw muscles. When they start . . . take cover!

At the 2016 London Six Day, he was clearly becoming more and more frustrated by the focus and questioning from reporters who seemed far more interested in his teammate, Bradley Wiggins. When Matt Rendell asked how he felt about watching Wiggo win the Derny race, in which Cav had ridden the first half earlier, he could barely contain his anger. The teeth became more firmly clenched and the jaw began to twitch. Then TV presenter OJ Borg asked him another question about his partner. Cav detonated a controlled explosion: 'I don't know. Why don't you just ask Bradley!? Everyone's just asking me questions about Brad. Haven't you got any questions to ask about me?' There was a second or two as some expletives hit the auditorium wall. Cue awkward laughter from OJ.

To be honest, I got off to a bad start with Mark. In fact, he blamed me for wrecking three months of his racing career. It all started with a viewer comment read out by my Eurosport colleague, David Harmon. Cav's teeth, it was said, looked like Bingo from the 1970s television programme

The Banana Splits Show. This character is a bright orange gorilla with rather prominent teeth. It was a light-hearted jibe, a bit of a tease, affectionate even. Just a humorous aside from a fan, if a little insensitive, but Cav took it personally. He was furious. What's worse is that he assumed the comment had come from me. Not surprising, as I'm given to a high degree of irreverence on occasion.

Now Cav is a handsome chap, so unknown to us was the fact that Mark had been teased about his dentition as a youngster at school. This latest episode pushed him to seek out corrective surgery to sort them out at the end of the season. He was going out with Miss Paraguay at the time, who recommended a local dentist. Rather than wait until he came home, Cav went for treatment. Sadly, the surgery didn't go well. He developed an infection, which resulted in further dental work and a huge dose of antibiotics that knocked out his early season prep. And I got the blame.

Our relationship continued to decline when I criticised his team's sprint leadout train at the Tour of Qatar in 2013. My job as a commentator is to give opinions. Opinions that can be right or wrong, but it is my job to comment and give my view – for what it's worth. The trouble is that there are times when you are going to be at odds with the riders who have given their best but failed. And if you have an opinion on that failure, firstly, they don't like it being highlighted if it's true; and secondly, if they think you're wrong, then obviously you're an absolute idiot.

During a sprint finale at the Tour of Qatar, I was calling it from inside of a truck with a low definition monochrome TV screen in front of me. The vision was terrible and I'd had to put a blanket over my head and TV monitor to be able to make anything out. Despite this, I could recognise the distinctive shape of Cav hunched over his handlebars in his classic sprint position, so I was focusing on him. I could see his lead out assemble, only for it to fall apart in the melée. It managed to get back together, only for it to be destroyed again and I said out loud as the bunch came to the approach: 'Wow, this is a mess.' The words I used were harsh but fair. I'm an emotive commentator and I say what I feel at the time. The truth is, I wanted him to win. Essentially I'm a fan and I was, I guess, voicing my own disappointment.

With a poor lead out, the inevitable happened and Cav didn't win the stage. Of course, he was livid, and as we know with Mark, he always reacts strongly when things don't go the way he wanted. Back at the hotel he watched the finish on TV and heard me call his race 'a mess', which of course made him even more furious.

The next sprint stage was a turnaround for him and the team. They won. When Mark saw our reporter Matt Rendell approaching, he said live on air, 'Right. Before we start, get that bloody Carlton Kirby down here, I'm going to give him a good slap.' Matt parried the suggestion with nervous laughter before carrying on with the interview.

It wouldn't be an understatement to say that, at this point in both our careers, Mark thought I was a bit of a git. It was an opinion that lingered. Indeed, we only began to build bridges a year later at the Tour of Turkey, when the organisers began harrying and bundling everyone into taxis for a long journey to the next stage start. I was in a car with fellow commentator Brian Smith when the door opened and, plop, Mark Cavendish sat down in the seat next to me. With a three- or four-hour drive ahead of us, I thought it best to clear the air.

'Hello, Mark,' I said. 'Are you still going to give me a bloody good slapping?'

Thankfully, there was to be no fat bleeding lip. Instead I had an enjoyable journey over three hours where we chatted affably about just about everything apart from the world of cycling. It was a key moment in our relationship and set a precedent for all our future encounters.

Being a Manxman, Mark knows a lot about motorbike racing. His home is famous for the Isle of Man TT races, which I've been commentating on for many years. Away from the pressures of our jobs, and stuck in a car for a few hours, we were able to shoot the breeze about motorbikes, Le Mans and fast cars. He was absolutely in his element. Mark is a petrolhead, with a collection of fast and powerful cars, including a McLaren with a unique Cavendish Green colour scheme and a Land Rover Desert Warrior with a 5.7-litre V10 Corvette engine. After the London Six Day, he was so hyped and driven by the adrenaline of racing that he spent the evening ferrying various people to the station, rumbling around in his 4 × 4, rattling all the windows of Stratford. Our children are of similar ages, which offers plenty of opportunity for non-cycling, no-pressure chats. It's now become a golden rule between us that, when we find ourselves in each other's company, however brief, we'll steer clear of the shop talk. It's nice, and a rare privilege, to get a window into the real Mark Cavendish.

To be the best, Mark Cavendish has had to be brutal and hide his kinder nature with an emotional suit of armour. He dons this before going into battle each day. What we see then is a precocious, at times demanding, egotistical and hugely ambitious Mark Cavendish. When the time inevitably comes for all the battles to have been fought and, for the most part, won, it will be a pleasure to see this approachable, considerate, polite and kind man emerge from the tumult.

BRADLEY WIGGINS

Tour de France compère: 'And now ladies and gentlemen, a word from the 2012 Tour de France Champion.'

Bradley Wiggins [*tapping mike*]: 'Have you all got your raffle tickets ready?'

Wiggins is a quick-change artist of the highest order. He's regularly altered his body shape to accommodate the disciplines he has mastered. He's an Olympic Champion track racer, an hour record holder, a Tour de France winner, a Monuments man, and a Time Trial World Champion.

His assault on the hour record took place on 7 June 2015. Some 6,000 spectators are crammed into what was London's Olympic Velodrome to experience a slice of cycling history as Bradley Wiggins limbers up in the track centre in preparation. Miguel Induráin, former record holder and Tour de France winner, is there as well as other sporting personalities you wouldn't normally see at a cycling event, like Seb Coe and Martin Johnson, captain of England's Rugby World Cup-winning team. I'm in the commentary box, working for Sky, who cheekily secured the broadcasting rights to the event. A series of build-up races have been keeping the public entertained and the clock ticks inexorably towards 6.30 p.m., the scheduled time for Bradley's start. Dame Sarah Storey is track centre doing interviews and due to join me on comms. With four minutes to go, I'm cued in for an ad break before the start of this historic attempt. An official tells Brad, 'Four minutes to go, Brad! OK?' But this is Bradley Wiggins, remember? And he doesn't always keep to the script. In the middle of the commercial break, which you can never cut away from, he decides that he's ready right now, he's reached the perfect place in his mind. He climbs on to his bike and, with no flowery build-up, nothing, bang! He's off!

The whole scenario was classic Bradley Wiggins: a highly driven, intensely focused maverick who does things the way he wants to do them and the rest of the world will just have to put up with that. The Sky on-site producer Doug Ferguson was in shock: 'Carlton – bin the intro, we are cutting live straight to you!' Off the break, the TV audience were met with a tumult in the velodrome: a Mexican wave of sound was following Brad around the track as I screamed: 'Bradley Wiggins waits for no man! He's already off!!!' Minutes later, Dame Sarah crashed into her position breathless after her dash from the infield. Chaos, Wiggo style, like it or lump it.

Bradley is an extraordinarily intense and quiet individual. He's always seemed ill at ease with the press and often claims he has been misquoted. He also reacts strongly to any perceived criticism. While Cavendish often oozes confidence, Bradley sometimes shows fragility. Like many great riders he is full of contradictions: he has the ability to take immense pain and to mentally divorce himself from the punishing physical demands of professional cycling, yet he also seems vulnerable. To cope on a Grand Tour, Bradley set his horizon close. He took one day at a time, yet he'd harboured a dream of winning the Tour de France since he was a schoolboy. And he did it!

Bradley can seem a bit rudderless and chaotic, but he responded brilliantly to the day-to-day plans of the Sky team strategists. And when he had this forensic guidance he was unstoppable.

To fully understand Bradley and the apparent sadness you see in his eyes, I think we have from consider his upbringing and parentage. He was born in Ghent, Belgium, the heartland of European cycling where his father, an Australian named Gary Wiggins, was a star of the Six Day racing scene. Wiggins senior had fantastic physical abilities but became a heavy drinker and a drug user, often using amphetamines to get him through races. He was based in England for a while and paired up with pursuit World Champion Tony Doyle, with whom he had a fair bit of success. Tony has told me that Gary was regularly using amphetamines by this time, and these, unsurprisingly, had a terrible effect on his personality and character. One day he and Tony were in the centre of the track in their Six Day cabin when a soigneur brought them their breakfast: oatmeal for Tony and cornflakes for Gary. Gary put his spoon into the bowl of cornflakes, took a mouthful and immediately spat the whole lot out. He then kicked over the table, including Tony's oatmeal, and screamed, 'Kellogg's! I said it had to be f--king *Kellogg's*!' He tore apart the booth, flinging bits of plywood all over the place and smashing anything he could find. All this because of the wrong brand of cornflakes.

Tony said that Gary was continually getting into fights for the slightest thing, from a security guard pointing out he'd forgotten his track pass to punch-ups in the pub over an accidental bump of elbows. Tony was too useful to him on track, so he was never going to be a target. 'And I was a big guy too,' says Tony. 'He didn't dare touch me.' Sadly for Gary, brawling was also the way he lost his life. He died of a head trauma after a fight at a party at Aberdeen in New South Wales. The investigation into his death never produced a conviction.

So it was that Bradley had little contact with his father and was raised by his mum in a council flat in Kilburn. He clearly inherited some pretty good cycling genes from his dad and he says, even now, that he respects him hugely as a cyclist, if not as a parent.

I've seen at first hand the warm, humble and shy side of Bradley. He will always do anything for the fans if not for the press. At the 2013 Giro, he was at the height of his fame, having won the Tour de France the year before. We were in Naples and I saw him get out of a taxi. He was walking over to say hello to me and Dan Lloyd when a huge bear of a man grabbed him and began hugging him, saying, 'Photo, photo.' There were minders all around trying to get the man to leave Brad alone, but the Tour de France star was compliant. Clearly it was the last thing he felt like doing, but he stood there while this guy started taking selfies with a queue of others forming behind him. Finally, the guy was happy, but before leaving the Tour de France winner in peace, he grabbed his shoulders and began planting huge, wet, sloppy kisses on each of his cheeks.

Said the fan, 'I respect you *so* much.' Mwah, mwah, mwah. 'So much respect!'

'Save some for yourself,' said Brad under his breath as he headed our way, wiping his cheeks.

Me: 'That fan seemed happy, Brad.'

Brad: 'It was like havin' a randy dog on your leg, FFS.'

Dan Lloyd [referring to Brad's shape ahead of the race]: 'You look good, Brad.'

Brad: 'You look like a f--king tourist.'

Dan Lloyd later binned the pink Giro sunglasses of which he'd been, until that moment, so proud.

With Dan wounded and me wary, we didn't say much more as we walked over a footbridge to a press conference in a castle.

I've walked alongside Bradley a few times like this, often in silence out of respect. But also because small talk is useless. Brad doesn't do small talk. And 'asking the bleedin' obvious' is just not on. Not that there would be a strong reaction if you did; you'd more likely get one of his deadeye looks. Which can feel worse.

Wiggins won the Tour in 2012, the first British man to do so, and he went on to win the gold medal in the Individual Time Trial at the London Olympics 12 days later. It was an amazing double and the very pinnacle of his career. His victory speech at the Tour was classic Brad. After opening with his jokey 'raffle tickets' line, he then spoke as a fan of the sport, talking about how much this meant to him and the unreality of it happening to a simple lad from a Kilburn housing estate. This humble man of the people went on to become a VIP, rubbing shoulders with celebrities and rock and roll greats. The contradictions were not lost on Bradley Wiggins himself. He said it was 'an unreal time'.

He was clearly struggling to come to terms with new goals and ambitions post-Tour. He'd made it clear that his triumph had been a one-off and that he had no intention of producing a series of similar victories, but it left him with a hole in his life. He certainly decided to give himself a pat on the back and embarked on a partying spree in the off season, including smoking the occasional cigarette, which made headlines. To me it seemed like a rebellion against all the rigours he had endured.

Sure enough, after a few weeks of partying and not riding a bike, the weight began to pile on. Belatedly Brad went to the gym to get back into shape. Sadly, he emerged after the close season 'gym fit' and muscle-bound;

not 'cycling fit' at all. He was well beyond even the Peter Sagan mould and simply too heavy to climb; a stark contrast to the previous season.

He was lost without a goal and he needed guiding. The focus had altered at Sky, with Chris Froome now chosen to lead the team into the next Tour de France. Brad duly entered the Giro but was in poor shape. Then, on a horrible, wet, cold day, a fear appeared to descend over him. He looked scared by the horrendous conditions on one of the descents. Everyone was terrified, including me. There followed a series of aquaplane crashes. Bradley pulled over to the side of the road and got off his bike. Sky said that he'd had a respiratory infection, but my reading of it was that he was both off form and pissed off. His team had moved focus to Froome, he wasn't race-winning fit and the weather was simply the last straw. I think he'd had enough.

It was time to reinvent himself. He initially thought the Monuments would be a good option, potentially Paris–Roubaix, and he did quite well, finishing ninth in 2014. But it was to the track he returned, where he had won a career tally of five Olympic golds. The hour record was the perfect project and goal for him to work on, and he turned himself around to once again achieve an amazing feat.

On 20 November 2016, Bradley returned to the city of his birth, Ghent, to partner Mark Cavendish in a Six Day, for what turned out to be the final run of his career. He spoke of remembering the smell of embrocation on the legs of the riders when he'd been there as a child, how it felt like coming home. On the very boards that his father had raced on 30 years earlier, Wiggo and Cav won the title – a fitting end to an extraordinary racing career. Once the formal interviews were over and the TV networks were off air, my co-commentator Tony Gibb and I hung back to watch. Brad took his time but finally held the auditorium mike and addressed the crowd, who'd packed into the track centre, where the celebrations were about to start. Deafening cheers rang out.

'Hold on, hold on, quiet for f--k's sake! I just want to say thanks to all of you and particularly to this man.' [*Gives Cav a shoulder hug.*] 'I couldn't have done this without him.' [*Cav starts to cry.*] 'I love this man and I love this place.'

That night, Cav went to bed early as Brad went to the nearby bar owned by the father of Six Day specialist Iljo Keisse and joined the attempt to drink the place dry. Two weeks later, Brad retired from all forms of cycling.

I often think of Sir Bradley as being more of a club rider in terms of his persona, rather than a star of the sport, which he certainly is. He'd probably take that as a compliment. He's what actors call the very best in their trade: 'a natural'.

CHRIS FROOME

Interviewer: 'It must be a pleasure to stuff all the criticism back down your detractors' throats?'

Chris Froome: 'I wouldn't put it quite like that, but yes, winning feels pretty good.'

If cucumbers could talk, they'd say 'as cool as a Froome'. A brilliant climber, expert time triallist and superb strategist, he's the ultimate cold-blooded competitor, who has won a remarkable four Tour de France yellow jerseys as well as the pink and red of the Giro and Vuelta – victory in Italy in May 2018 meant he wore all three at the same time. Chris seemingly has no inner demons. He himself is the demon. Just ask any member of the French press corps. Or indeed any rider.

Polite to a fault and quietly spoken he may well be, but he's dogged. His nickname is Froome-Dog. A fitting moniker to wrap around the most single-minded, ambitious, dedicated and committed rider of his generation, perhaps of all time.

Froome's public persona is, to be honest, a marketing man's worst nightmare, but a PR man's dream. He comes across as very 'safe' if not a little bland. You don't expect to hear any expletives from Chris. Of course, when he's interviewed in public he is nearly always accommodating and diplomatic. His replies generally toe the party line, as he is so well briefed. This is a very bright man, who is very conscious of the consequences of his words. When he's in PR mode, he gives away nothing. He thanks his teammates for the great job they did on the day, he'll pay respect to his rivals and fashion a modest outlook on his prospects in the race. Everything he says is safe, couched within standard responses.

In person he's more convivial and charming than he comes across on TV, but he's not exactly chummy. The character that he presents to the world, his public persona, is a construct, a facade that hides the traits of a cold-blooded, calculated competitor, a man with hidden depths and passions who has overcome illness to become the most dominating cyclist of his generation. Domination is the key word here: his force of personality has enabled him to overpower rivals, both within and outside of his team, in his quest to be the best. He is the most decorated of our heroes: a four-time Tour de France champion, he has six Grand Tour titles in total and at one point held all three – the Tour, Vuelta and Giro – at the same time. Simply remarkable.

When paratroopers train, they do so in full kit with a rucksack on their back. When they take the kit off, they can run for another 16km (10 miles). Chris Froome trained for years with a similar handicap without even knowing it. He discovered in 2010 that he'd contracted bilharzia from swimming in a lake in Africa. Known as river blindness, it's an infection caused by a parasitic worm that lives in water in the tropics. The parasite can remain in the body for many years, causing damage to bladder, kidneys and liver.

From his arrival at Sky in 2010 until his startling ascension in the 2011 Vuelta, Froome suffered a grey patch of results that were so dismal his team were considering letting him go. Jonathan Vaughters was lining him up to join his team at Garmin. Froome puts his poor performance down to the effects of bilharzia, which weakened him and left him incapable of reaching his true potential until it was finally diagnosed at the end of 2010. The parasite feeds on red blood cells, making his body less capable of storing oxygen – a significant performance hurdle. Even after treatment he succumbed to a series of chest infections because the illness had damaged the immune system of his body.

Once cured, he began to assemble a series of remarkable results. Rather like the paratroopers shedding their backpacks, Froome was suddenly able to perform without the effects of a debilitating condition he'd carried for so long. He was free.

If you look at Froome's physique and body shape in the 2016 Tour, it's remarkably different from the chubby, baby-faced kid who was trying to make an inroad into the world of professional cycling seven or eight years prior. Back in his Barloworld racing team days, he was 9kg (20lb) heavier – and he looked it. Froome has succeeded in shedding every ounce of spare body fat without affecting his power output. Now he not only shows remarkable staying power in the mountains but is also one of the best time triallists in the peloton. Once criticised for his poor bike-handling and descending skills, he's now winning stages of the Tour de France by exploiting others' weaknesses coming down the mountains.

But perhaps more remarkable than his physical attributes and impressive skills set is his sheer strength of will. He has used this to impose himself on both his team and the pro peloton. In 2012 he was employed as a super-domestique in support of his team leader, Bradley Wiggins, who indeed went on to win the Tour de France.

Problems started during the race as the pair climbed La Toussuire. Brad was in yellow, more than two minutes ahead of Froome in the General Classification (GC), but Froome was clearly frustrated. Feeling in the form of his life, he suddenly put in an attack on the leading group, which included his team leader, Wiggins. Within seconds he'd created a gap of more than 30m (100ft) and Bradley was clearly struggling. There was no way that Wiggo could keep up with his supposed domestique, the man whose job it was to guide him up the mountains. Back in the team car, Sky race director David Brailsford was going crazy on the radio, ordering Froome to fall back and support Bradley. The theatrics with which Froome responded were so over the top it reminded me of a bad mime artist. There are subtle ways of getting on to your radio, but he almost ripped his shirt off, holding out the under-jersey radio mike for the whole world to see. There he was, still powering up the mountain, one-handed, looking behind him almost in disbelief at the faltering climbing abilities of his supposed team leader. It was a clear message that he was the stronger rider of the two, and that he was capable of taking the yellow jersey himself.

In the aftermath, Team Sky put their PR faces on to cover up what was clearly a move from Froome that was way beyond any team orders. But Froome still wanted to make a further point: on Stage 17 in the Pyrenees, he again went ahead of Wiggins and started to make frequent glances back at his teammate, pulling ahead while gesturing for him to hurry up and join him. As Laurent Jalabert, the retired former Tour winner, said at the end of the stage, 'It wasn't a beau geste. . . You don't do that to your teammates. I think it darkens the triumph of Wiggins.'

Back in the Sky bus at the end of the day, it was chaos. Bradley was threatening to pull out of the Tour. Brailsford was battling to control the situation. Both stars had to be appeased. Froome was clearly the stronger; Brad was on the edge. Time for some masterly management. Whatever happened in the bus that day remains secret. But order was restored. How financial this settlement became was a matter of huge debate and speculation among the journalists. What was clear, however, was that this was the day Froome became Team Leader in Waiting. They rode on. Froome toed the line. Brad won the race.

Froome's behaviour was not soon forgotten by Wiggins.

The sheer brazen impudence of Froome's actions were in stark contrast to the face he puts on in front of the media. The choirboy looks hide a brute within who will employ almost any tactics to impose his will on those around him. What's almost scary is the cold, calculated way in which he does so.

Froome's intelligence and skill at manipulating the rules were highlighted again in the 2014 Tour, where we could see him planning on the hoof too. Occasionally this has to be defensive. The riders were coming to the end of a stage and within the 20km (12-mile) limit of not being allowed assistance of any kind from the team cars. These are rules designed to make racing safer so that bidons and feed bags are not bouncing around and hampering a climax. Froome had, for once, miscalculated his food intake and was heading for the cyclist's nightmare – 'the bonk', where all energy suddenly drains away because of a lack of nutrition. Froome raised his hand to indicate a technical issue such as a puncture. The commissaire radioed for the Team Sky car to come forward to assist. There was no puncture. Instead, Geraint Thomas went back to the car and collected gels. Chris was faltering as Thomas quickly returned. Seeing what had happened, the race director went apoplectic. Froome was taking the risk that the only sanction would be a fine, nothing more severe. The fact is that Froome, even in extremis, had the nous to read the situation and dealt with it, albeit by bending the rules on feeding so late in the race. This is genius.

While Froome plays the diplomat in press conferences, he's not averse to approaching journalists to put his view across in a more uncompromising fashion. And with some force. He texts me occasionally. In the 2013 Vuelta a España, on the opening kilometres of a tough climbing day, he crashed into a barrier on the side of the road, the type that blend gently into the ground. They were not immediately obvious and should have been pennanted by a race steward. Sure enough, Froome crashed into them. I commented at the time that this could have been as a result of his head-down riding style, which has him contemplating his handlebars. It's a position he seems to be comfortable riding in and has been noted by many. Froome battled through the stage but was later forced to pull out of the race with a foot injury. At the end of the day, when he heard what I'd said, he was furious and sent this message:

'If you didn't see the crash yourself please reserve your opinions. It wasn't a "lack of vision" as you pointed out as often as you could today. I was pushed into the barrier.'

Sure enough, there were pictures that came out later which proved I was right. But the only way we were ever going to speak to him again that race was if I apologised. I texted back two replies:

'To be fair, at the time I said it was an assumption and we could be wrong. I'm a huge fan and wish you the very best. Hope you race on well. Fond regards.'

'I'll say something on air today.'

His reply: 'Thanks Carlton, I'd appreciate that. The last thing I need right now is media reporting that "I wasn't looking where I was going" or similar.'

The next day, on air, I said that Froome had claimed that it had been a racing incident and that the viewers could draw their own conclusions.

What Froome presents is a polished persona, but on the inside there's a demon. The convivial diplomat that we see in a pre- or post-race interview is dumped unceremoniously in the bin as soon as he climbs aboard the Sky bus or his bike. He is actually anything but bland. Froome does whatever has to be done.

GERAINT THOMAS

Interviewer: 'How did you do that?'

Geraint Thomas: 'Honestly, I have absolutely no idea!'

Clever, cuddly, classy. Everybody loves Geraint. A cycling god you can worship without having to justify your religion. When anyone says: 'I love G', nobody ever asks why. People know a good guy when they see one. And we've seen a lot of this multiple Olympic and World track champion. Oh, and did I mention he won the Tour de France?

Geraint Thomas has always been one of the more colourful individuals in the peloton with his witty ripostes to reporters and tongue-in-cheek comments after hard-fought battles in the Tour, Giro and Vuelta. Along with Bradley Wiggins and Mark Cavendish, he brings a bit of British dry humour to the continental scene, in stark contrast to the far more serious Froome and the evasive Simon Yates.

Geraint is a grounded guy who loves his rugby and football. Given this, it's easy to forget what a phenomenal cyclist he is. His status as wingman to Froome in the Grand Tours means we often forget that he's a successful double Olympic gold medallist and three-time World Champion on the track in the brutal event of the team pursuit.

Growing up in rugby-mad Cardiff, he had to endure his fair share of teasing from his contemporaries to whom he had to justify shaving his legs and wearing Lycra bib shorts. But his early success with local club Maindy Flyers set him on the path to cycling glory. Like many of our British road racing stars – Wiggo, Cav and Yates – he found initial success on the track.

The fact is that G is just the sort of guy you'd want in the highly pressurised environment of an Olympic cycling team, to lighten up the atmosphere with a quip before the most important race of your career. He has developed a mindset over the years to overcome that excruciating fear, paranoia and sickening anxiety before these huge moments: he focuses on the process, not the outcome, and reverts to what he calls the computer in his head, programmed by coach Steve Peters. Off the track, there are times he lets the computer default to daft. He once put out a rumour that one of Team Sky's secrets to success was to eat only onions for one day a week. Some professionals missed the mischief in this and took his comment at face value. There are no methane-powered bikes, but that month we did wonder.

What we all love about G is that he is so down to earth. He doesn't overcomplicate things. He once said, 'At the end of the day, we just train hard, rest well, eat well – and that's it. It's just hard work and I think sometimes they think we must be doing some crazy new diet or crazy new training regime, but it's pretty simple.' So keep him well serviced, fill him up, point him out of the bus and off he goes. 'Nothing complicated.' Believe me, in the complicated world of team road cycling this view is as refreshing as it comes.

He likes to party and has been known to fully enjoy his time off the bike. Beers, burgers and Welsh cakes – he tweeted that the baked delicacies were the only way to celebrate after winning the Tour de France. But all this ignores the fact that he's led an incredibly disciplined life since the age of nine, when he began to take cycling seriously.

Like a lot of professional cyclists, he's an absolute hardman. He ruptured his spleen in a crash back in 2005 and raced with a fractured pelvis in 2013 on nothing more than ibuprofen. His crash on the 2015 tour, when he was wrapped around a telegraph pole on the descent of Col de Manse, was a classic G moment. To everyone who saw it, it looked like an horrendous crash, one likely to have horrible consequences. G, though, clambered back up the mountainside and remounted his bike, his only complaint that he'd lost a pair of his trademark white sunglasses. 'I feel all right for now,' he explained at the finish line. 'I guess my doctor will ask me my name soon. I'll say: Chris Froome.'

He's been beset by bad luck on the few occasions when he's been let off the leash. His first attempt as a general classification Grand Tour contender ended when he smashed into a badly parked police motorbike on the Giro. For any rider to suffer injury and have to bow out from a race is disappointing, but given how few chances he'd had beforehand, you might have expected him to be devastated that his opportunity was dashed by a badly parked bike. G simply pulled himself together and carried on chipping away, waiting for the moment to come.

That moment duly arrived in 2018, when Froome's form never fully recovered from his victory at the Giro. Sky said that Thomas had always been their Plan B, but the truth was that there'd never been any properly considered strategy other than that Froome should win a fifth Tour title to equal the extraordinary record of cycling greats Jacques Anquetil, Eddy Merckx, Bernard Hinault and Miguel Induráin. Plan G was that he'd be Froome's wingman. That all changed when the leader got dropped.

G's victory was incredibly popular and restored a bit of faith in professional cycling. Unlike many of the other riders, he's never been tainted by any insinuations of drug-taking. He's never considered applying for a Therapeutic Use Exemption, for example. He's clean in a way that must surely disappoint many rabid story-hunters.

In all my time around the peloton and press rooms, I can't recall that anyone has ever had a bad word to say about G. Which is not to say he's boring or squeaky clean. He's his own man and that takes belief. Belief in himself. It's this mindset that really counts.

Henry Ford once said: 'Whether you think you can, or whether you think you can't . . . you're right.'

So, believe.

'Just dream big,' G said after his Tour de France win. 'Go for it. There's nothing holding you back. You can have ups and downs, but if you believe in something, keep the faith, keep fighting. And don't let people put you down.'

I'll drink to that!

SIMON YATES

Interviewer: 'Tell me about your plans today.'

Simon Yates: 'I'll get on the bike and try and win. What do you want me to say?'

Ever had the feeling you've seen somebody before? Simon is half of the Yates phenomenon. Like his near-identical twin brother, Adam, he speaks as fast as his legs go round. And that … is about all we know. 'I'm not one of your cycling mega stars, OK? I just ride my bike.' Reluctant he may be, but he is a cycling mega star, having won La Vuelta in 2018.

When the Yates twins opted to sign with Orica–GreenEDGE (now Mitchelton–Scott) rather than Sky back in 2014, manager Dave Brailsford knew at the time that he'd missed a trick. Simon was already a World Champion gold medal winner on the track, who'd roomed with Chris Froome at the Commonwealth Games at the tender age of 18, while his brother, Adam, was making a name for himself both at home and on the continent as a road racer. Four years later, Sir Dave, the architect of Britain's cycling success on the track and road, was probably really annoyed he'd failed to add yet another winning rider to his roster. He made the mistake of making an offer just for Simon. Fed up with being separated, Adam and Simon decided to sign up for the Australian team instead, because its offer was for both riders and not just one.

Adam and Simon's decision to move to the smaller, less well-paid team from the southern hemisphere has been a good one for the boys from Bury. Team boss Matt White has nurtured and groomed them for great things. If they'd gone to Sky, they could have ended up as another pair of super-domestiques in the mould of Peter Kennaugh, Luke Rowe or Ben Swift. Geraint Thomas spent 10 years riding alongside Froome – two seasons at Barloworld and eight at Sky – before he was truly let off the leash in a Grand Tour race that involved them both. Even then, it came down to circumstance at the 2018 Tour rather than design on the part of his team. It was only when Froome's amazing run of consecutive Grand Tour wins finally crept up on him and his form suffered that Thomas was allowed to fly. Two unclipped pairs of wings were handed to the Yates brothers at Mitchelton–Scott. They flew.

Simon and Adam began their bike racing careers as kids when their father introduced them to the track at Manchester velodrome. They trained on the moors outside their home in Bury, each brother pushing the other on with a similar sibling rivalry to that displayed by the Brownlee brothers in triathlon – sibling rivalry is a powerful thing. Being one and two in the pecking order is nice for the family. But nicest of all is being Number One at the dinner table.

The Yates brothers' talent was spotted early, but it was only Simon who secured an Olympic Academy draft. Adam went off to France to work his way through the junior team system on the continent while Simon had a more structured beginning in the academy. Both developed well, emerging from their differing approaches to the pro ranks with parallel success at the Tour de France in the white jersey competition. In 2016 Adam was first to win the Young Rider Classification, finishing a remarkable fourth in the full overall ranking. The following year Simon also took the white jersey and finished seventh in the general classification. So the race was on for them to take a full Grand Tour title. Nobody could figure out who would cross that line first. It was a tight call, but in 2018 attention focused on Simon. He went very close at the Giro d'Italia, leading the race before he went too deep and faltered. He finally made it home with victory at the Vuelta a España where, appropriately, brother Adam was his main domestique.

For Simon, success began on the track, but it wasn't long before he was making a name for himself on the road as well. With his diminutive build, he was a born climber, but that heritage of track cycling reveals an inner strength and power that means he can sprint and time trial too, as proven in the 2019 Paris–Nice. Placing himself in the teens on stage races, he was getting Top 10 finishes very soon, including a seventh place overall at the 2017 Tour de France, cementing his place as team leader and GC contender. And then came 2018.

Given his achievements, it's remarkable that he wasn't a massive superstar with his face plastered all over billboards up and down the country. You know: 'Simon Yates likes Tunnock's Caramel, the biscuit of Champions' – that sort of thing.

2018 was an astonishing year for Simon Yates. First up was the Giro, where he displayed the full range of aggressive fighting chutzpah that had the cycling cognoscenti, if not the British public, dropping their jaws at the sheer impudence of this kid. Smashing heavyweights up the Dolomites and the Alps, he was in pink, and winning stages with verve, strength and racing acumen, steadily building up a healthy lead with bonus seconds whenever he could get them. And then he blew up. While Chris Froome was putting in the ride of his life on the Finestre, the ride of a century even, Simon lost almost 39 minutes and the lead that fateful afternoon. Exhausted, spent and used up, he could barely finish the stage and was nursed to the finish line by his teammates.

Fast-forward four months and Yates arrived at the Vuelta a more mature rider. Still aggressive, yes, but having learned his lesson in the Italian spring, he knew now to race within himself, pace himself and play the long game. Added to his individual success was the remarkable fact that his eventual victory in Spain meant that, for the first time ever, all the holders of the three Grand Tours for that year were different riders of the same nationality. A magnificent roster of Brits, with Simon Yates' Vuelta win completing the feat.

How extraordinary, then, that he has gone largely unnoticed by the British general public. This may well be because the nation has simply grown tired of cycling after all the dark and murky stories surrounding the sport. Or it may have been general 'sports fatigue', what with the Winter Olympics demanding attention in the early months and the FIFA World Cup making a nuisance of itself mid-season. Who knows? But the nation's lack of attention may well have had something to do with the personality of Simon Yates himself.

Public relations work is not Simon's forte. Like many a GC rider, he is supremely focused on his racing. He seems to see his role as winning bike races – and nothing else. His clipped responses to media questions and the general public don't help the overwhelming impression that he really can't be bothered with the whole PR circus. His lack of engagement means there is not yet an affectionate public nickname attached to this cycling superstar – Froome-Dog, Wiggo, Cav and G all trip off the tongue.

Whether Simon Yates likes it or not, it's headlines on the sports pages and internet that help to generate the funding of his sport and indeed the very team that pays his wages. Now he's got a Grand Tour under his belt, let's hope that he opens up a bit and shows a more human side. At only 26 years old, he's going to be on podiums at the biggest bike races in the world for some time yet. Hopefully he'll be willing to share a bit more of himself along the way.

6
KELLY'S SMALLS

10.15 a.m. I am at the edge of the TV compound where I wait in line for a bag check. Sean Kelly offers up his tatty SPORT bag and is immediately waved through inspection. This bag is the sort of carrier that any normal kid would be bullied about at school: tatty, faded, red and ripped. Its holes are 'good ventilation for me wet stuff'. Kelly does not waste money on bags, or indeed a laundry service. He does his own each night. I am highly familiar with Kelly's smalls. Security know about them, too – which I'm convinced is why they wave him through. Nobody wants to rummage through that lot. A more likely reason for Kelly's wave-by is that he is The King and he would not be expected to cause any trouble. I, however, am of far lesser renown. Usually for me it's a rather cursory inspection. Nothing serious save for the regular, 'What is this?'

'It's a stapler,' I say.

I have to show them. It's my own fault. I bought a stapler that looks a bit like a gun, especially to scanners. I should get another, but it's very efficient and I've had it ages. A bit like Kelly's bag. 'Ah, un agrafeur!' Oui, indeedy. Thankfully, after about a week of seeing me looking forlorn as Kelly waltzes through, they give me one of the prized possessions of any tour: the Trusted Bag tag to bypass this search. But before I am elevated to this status I have a couple of days of bag rummaging, and sometimes the testicle scan too. I'm referring to the handheld detector unit seen at airports. They say this is for the belt buckle area, but I think otherwise. To be honest, if I were doing this for a job I'd scan some privates and give 'em a nudge too, just for a laugh. TV compound Gate Security is a boring job, so you have to mix it up a bit.

Slightly less comfortable, I head inside the high-fenced compound. Here you are a little freer than the general public, who are denied entry. You still have the men with radios in their ears, the most inanimate of whom are the VIP heavies. These guys become visibly heavier, as in more threatening, on elevated security VVIP days, such as a presidential visit.

**'I QUITE LIKE THE GERMAN KIT AS WELL,
BUT DON'T TELL MY GRANDAD.'**

7
CIGARETTES AND COFFEE

10.30 a.m. I am looking for our commentary position. Kelly has wandered off, looking for the Eurosport light production area, where the crew gather and keep their gear, snacks and so on. It's an informal rest zone with plastic chairs where you can also watch the output on a tabletop TV. This is always something of an artistic creation, thrown together in urgency so the coffee machine can be fired up ASAP. For our mostly French production staff, an espresso and a cigarette is a morning essential – or, as they call it, breakfast. Everything else is simply chucked about. Cameras and newspapers mix with half-eaten baguettes, drying T-shirts, edit cases, Greg LeMond's mobile air-con unit, biscuits, sun cream and the usual camping ephemera. It's not pretty, but Kelly finds it comfy and settles in with a copy of *L'Équipe*.

It's all very different for Eurosport's regular neighbours inside the compound: the American NBC Sport team. Everyone knows the massive vehicles belong to them, not just because of the huge lettering on the sides of these behemoths but also because they have been corralled, in the style of a John Wayne western, into their own metal village.

Security often guide broadcasters sharing the same language on to pitches next to each other. I guess this is so that, should they have to shout: 'Get your head down!' in the English-speaking area, everyone would understand and act immediately. Except, that is, for Jens Voigt, who works for NBC; they're rather fond of him and his motto: 'Shut up legs!' The Jensie would, after such an order, naturally drift into the pedantry of an accomplished German student of English: 'Excuse me, but if you mean *hide* or *get on the floor*, would it not be better to say so precisely? I mean "Get your head down" can mean *to have a sleep*, can it not? This is just my suggestion.' The Jensie speaks great English, which is why NBC employ him, but he can get rather literal.

The Americans, of course, take everything very seriously indeed. They don't have their own security and, frankly, they don't need it because they operate in a massive metal prison. It's like their own sanitised village. It's got everything in there. The French admire this: 'Their coffee machines are permanent. Wow!' They also have showers, wardrobe, make-up, lounges, catering, production and edit suites. All highly ordered and out of bounds. You can often catch a glimpse of legendary commentator Phil Liggett in the sunshine on the top floor of one of their three-storey pantechnicons having a fruit smoothie before make-up. Paul Sherwen, his former colleague and one-time pro, used to toss down peanut M&Ms as if feeding chimps. 'There you go, peasants!' he'd shout down, followed by his trademark yak-yak-yak guffaw. And we were grateful; just one more reason why he'll be so missed. Paul provided a glorious dose of irreverence in a world of egos. No matter what your rank, you were treated the same. Everyone was a target for his mischief but universally took no offence.

The only other contact between NBC and Eurosport France comes in the form of complaints about drifting cigarette smoke. This is a regular thing. The way the Americans engage electric fans and shutters against a mere whiff of Eurosport's tobacco smoke, you'd think it was a gas attack. I've never seen men in pressed chinos and polo shirts get so agitated.

BOMB SQUAD

Meanwhile, as Kelly reads *L'Équipe* amid the mayhem of Eurosport International, I am at the finish line installing myself for the day ahead. I have passed the final checkpoint, which is a visual once-over made by the bearded and well-hewn chief engineer, Matthieu. I can now go about my business – except, of course, in the eventuality of *une operation exceptionelle* being declared. In other words: dogs!

Bomb dogs have great fun. Their life is a game of hide-and-seek. They are the jolly end of the police dog division. Their unit naturally includes guard dogs and attack dogs, usually in the shape of Dobermanns or German shepherds. Bomb dogs, on the other hand, are almost exclusively spaniels. They don't look very policey. They also smell very doggy in a glandular sort of way, and, due to the fact that they know there is a treat coming very soon, they get very excited. And when they get excited it gets even more pheromonal. You see, even if they do not find a rogue device they will get a biscuit. They love their job. I always wonder if these reward biscuits smell like Semtex. It would make sense. Anyway, as the game goes on, the spaniel is encouraged to go just about everywhere. The sniffing-out job is given to this particular breed because it has an enormous capacity to smell. Its nasal passages are cavernous. Sadly, such a sniffing void has a good deal of snot up there too. Scent glands need moisture to work properly, and sometimes this is shared with everyone who happens to be in the proximity of a series of blowouts that balance the sniffing. It's rank. Of course, all this can be going on while we are on air. Bomb dogs' operations are random.

Keeping tabs on a race can be something of a challenge at the best of times, but a panting dog with both his front and back end happy glands in meltdown can be a distraction. Add to the mix the presence of commentator staples like sandwiches and bars of chocolate, and you have trouble. Sean Kelly has lost the occasional *sandwich mixte* to these hounds while our German colleagues in the booth opposite once looked through the partition glass holding a newly shortened knackwurst and displaying a forlorn expression that asked 'Was ist das?' Worst of all, though, is the fact that a happy dog in hunting mode can get very waggy. You can bet that during a commentary if you hear the conversation go something like: '. . . and hEEEre we go jUUUst approaching the tUUUUUUrn for the col . . .', you can be sure there is a sniffer dog's tail doing battle with a broadcaster's testicles.

'FOR THOSE OF YOU LISTENING ON TWITTER, THIS IS A CYCLE RACE.'

8
CARJACK

10.45 a.m. We have been cleared as a zone of safety. Kelly has arrived and is asking what the smell is. 'Spaniels,' I explain. Then just as he is setting up, his phone goes. It's security. The conversation at his end goes like this: 'Hello. . . Yes. Yes, it is. . . Ooooh, right. . . Right ho! Yep. . . Right ho. Sorry. Yep. Oooookay.'

'Everything OK, Sean?' I venture.

'I've got to shift the car.'

Then a drawn-out 'F--k sake!' for good measure.

Every authorised car has a banner sticker on the front and back screens, which features a unique number. These stickers are naturally highly prized and impossible to rip off; although plenty have been shredded as fans try to pull a fast one, with the idea of pinching a sticker and getting closer to the action than they're allowed. Cars are badged so that if the vehicle is in a place that it should not be, a warning can be issued. Should this warning go unheeded, the car will be banned for all or part of the race.

So all warnings regarding parking are to be heeded immediately. Sean disappears.

MORE SECURITY THAN SPECTATORS

Let's briefly move from the overzealous security to overkill, shall we? Keeping any Grand Tour secure is a tough challenge. The nature of racing on open roads, covering vast distances each day, means it is perhaps the most vulnerable form of sport there is. It is simply impossible to police an active event that on some days spans more than 200km (125 miles). The modern world is a dangerous place and so every effort is made to keep the most vulnerable parts of a race on open roads secure.

There are three types of area requiring stringent security measures: the start, the finish and any pinch points where the race will slow and crowds will naturally gather – usually big mountain tests and populous towns and villages.

So security tends to be selective or, rather, concentrated in the potential danger zones.

The only exception to this I have come across was the Tour of Beijing – remarkable in the depth and breadth of its security operation, but also dead because of it.

The race had clearly been kept secret from the population to avoid what worried the organisers most: crowds.

For mile after mile, all you witnessed was a highly policed urban desert. The riders were the omega men, apparently the last on the planet, save for a very lucky few. Hardly anyone actually saw the race on site . . . eerie!

Even the police at the roadside didn't see what passed by; they were duty-bound to actively observe an alleyway, for example, to which they had been posted. This meant they stood with their backs to the road where the action was. Thousands of them, it seems, all spaced out at various 'danger' points with their backs to the race, guarding every side road, junction and pedestrian crossing you can imagine. They were like statues bolt upright with their overlarge breadboard hats sloping at an hors catégorie angle extending down past the top of their shoulders.

All this prompted an obvious question: Why bother to have the ultimate spectator sport come to your country and not allow spectators? I asked one of the security people. A little nonplussed, he explained it was to keep the race secure. It wasn't about entertaining the masses; it was about showing the best of the country to a worldwide audience 'without interference' – from the general public, obviously. Well, thanks for the view of the magnet factory! Save for that, I can honestly say I can't remember a single majestic vista, or anything else for that matter, that would tempt a TV viewer into making the trip.

The Beijing Tour no longer exists.

'MY GRAN SAID NOTHING COOLS YOU LIKE A CUP OF TEA. SHE WAS NUTS.'

9
COMFORT BREAKS

11.00 a.m. Time to go racing. But first. . .

As the Queen Mother, God bless her soul, reportedly once said, 'Never walk past a loo and never refuse a cup of tea.'

I would say that's a pretty good rule for both rider and commentator alike. But what goes in must also come out and there have been numerous occasions when both professional bike riders and commentators have been caught short, either finding themselves low on vital sustenance or indeed rather urgently needing the famous comfort break. Now, if you're going to spend say five hours of your time riding or commentating on a full stage, you'll definitely need to relieve yourself at some point. With this always in mind, the first thing I do when I arrive at the TV compound is to look for the pissoir. A rather public but very handy plastic urinal. A very big one. This monstrosity can accommodate five proud male journalists standing in a circle, who, on cool days, regularly chat while doing what they have to do. The women's cubicle facility is less congenial but apparently better smelling. Anyway, it is rather essential that this upright plastic receptacle is located close at hand if you want to take advantage of an ad break; I would say within 20m (65ft) of the commentary box door would be ideal. If it's any further away, it can be a devil to find in the maze of trucks and cables that make up any media park. I have known Kelly to go on a walkabout in desperate search of relief and I'll be left jabbering away on my own for 20 minutes or so. On hot tours – let's say La Vuelta, where temperatures regularly exceed 35°C (95°F) – these pissoirs can become rank. Conversation around them dries up as the wafts of ammonia gas from the exit fluid produced by numerous beery journalists and engineers billows invisibly around those seeking relief. It makes the eyes water.

'What's wrong!?'

'It's OK, I'm not crying. I've been for a piss.'

'Ahh.'

Meanwhile, out on course things are a little more freestyle for the riders.

It's amazing how many times I've been asked the question, 'How do the riders go to the toilet?' Well, when you gotta go, you gotta go! The comfort break has produced various public displays that the cameras and picture editors alike are, on the whole, pretty good at keeping away from broadcast.

THE START LINE

The start line of a stage on a Grand Tour can be a nerve-jangling time for the riders. Even on the last day of the Tour de France, which is a rather processional affair until the peloton reach Paris, the sprinters will be on edge because this is the most prestigious stage for them to win. The unofficial Sprint World Championships, even. But each day has something worth fighting for: a breakers' day, a climbers' day and so on. Any start line is time to go to work. Don't forget that professional racing is, at its core, a form of combat. Sure, everyone will have emptied their bladders before the off, but the actual racing won't start until the so-called départ fictif has been completed – and that can take some time. Everyone is fully hydrated before the start of this processional roll-out. This gives the riders a chance to warm up on the move and the fans at the departure venue a look at the riders. It also gives all competitors and teams a chance to check that the bikes are set correctly before racing begins proper at the départ réel, aka Kilometre Zero. This parade can be rather long if there's a big city to be negotiated before they get out on more open roads. Sometimes there are promotional reasons for a delay before the true start: the riders may be guided through an industrial park passing a major sponsor's factory or such like. If this happens to be a full commentary day from start to finish, this false start can be purgatory: 'And there is the Wash-Easy complex . . . the largest producer of industrial launderette machines in Turkey . . . it says here.'

Once they're up to speed and the director is happy with the way everything is going, he'll stick his head out of the sunroof of the leading car, wave his flag and finally they'll be off. But often not for long.

If it's a sprinter's stage, a breakaway will quickly be allowed to form – and this is the perfect time for the peloton to take a pee. It allows the breakaway to build up a decent buffer and the rest of the pack to do their business at the side of the road. It's not shown on TV very often, except by accident. It's not a pretty sight. Sometimes the race leader or the patron of the peloton (a senior and well respected rider) will flamboyantly come to the front and drift to the side of the road. It's a cue to everyone who needs to go to stop at the side of the road, pull aside their bibs and try to avoid the spray from anyone else. Difficult on a breezy day. All this is supposed to be away from the gaze of the public. Indeed, there are rules about this. And fines. Basically, don't do it in town or at a place where the crowd is dense. If you do, carefully worded edicts will be issued along with a fine. These contraventions vary in terms of their official description (often euphemistic), depending on the race. They are detailed in the course road book and can be quite hilarious.

'Not respecting the sobriety and conduct expected of a rider.'

'Bringing the race into disrepute.'

Or even once: 'Public display of intimate body parts.'

Take your pick, but basically they all mean a fine for getting your knob out in public. Or, indeed, your lady bits. Fines will follow and are documented in a list of shame the following day as part of the results dossier. We always flip to the back page for a giggle at the Naughty List.

Sean Kelly's An Post team was once racing the Tour of Britain while we were commentating on the Vuelta out in Spain, and Sean was sent an email from his Directeur Sportif back home saying that they'd been 'unfairly fined' by the organisers. Apparently an angry resident had complained about a couple of the guys peeing over his hedge. Later, it turned out not to have been any of the team's riders at all but those in the team car itself. This was, of course, hilarious to us as Kelly shouted down the phone, 'What's wrong with a sales rep's toilet?' Otherwise known as using a regular drink bottle, this is the sort of thing you encounter in lay-bys all over the world. I used to wonder why the bright orange soft drink Irn-Bru was often dumped half-finished by the road. Well, it's not Irn-Bru.

Of course, the subject of toilet breaks came sharply into focus at the 2017 Giro, when Tom Dumoulin got his feeding all wrong and found that he needed to evacuate his system. The fact that this happened to be while he was wearing the leader's jersey in a Grand Tour in front of millions of viewers, just as the peloton was about to tackle an iconic climb, was rather unfortunate. The cameras could not ignore the race leader at such a crucial and potentially decisive moment, no matter what the reason. It was the story, however scatological. Tom Poomoulin was a briefly popular nickname.

To avoid this sort of thing happening, cyclists have, over the last century, tried to refine a feeding system that avoids such embarrassing and potentially race-losing situations. There are many things to eat that are carb specific and, not to put too fine a point on it, don't produce stools.

A favoured snack is a ball of rice, often dipped in honey. Rice is amazing: it is almost entirely metabolised by the human body, being so finely broken down that it generates the maximum amount of energy while leaving very little waste. If you get your feed wrong, however – by taking on too much fibre, say – you can get a problem later, which is exactly what happened to poor old Tom.

At the famous moment I was sitting next to my co-commentator Dan Lloyd, and at first I couldn't work out what was going on. I could see him pulling to the side of the road and getting off the bike and I said, 'He's got a problem.' He took off his helmet and then the top came off, the leader's jersey, and I still had no idea what he was doing. Dan Lloyd, who has some experience of this kind of thing himself, being a former racer, blurted out, 'Oh no! Oh *no*! Not *that*!' Dan understood as soon as the helmet came off. You have to take the helmet off to get the jersey off. And the jersey has to come off to get the shorts down, which are normally held in place by looped braces under the jersey.

'Not what?' I asked as the whole process began to unfold. Dan silently mouthed the word *shit* at me before imploring the cameras to leave Tom alone. The camera operator hadn't realised either. Thank heavens the director did; so most blushes were saved. As the shorts came down we cut to another shot – though for a split second or two we got to see more of Tom Dumoulin than even his mother has seen in recent years.

Tom took all the resulting jibes with a smile and a sense of humour. Pictures appeared on the internet of bikes with loos attached to the saddle. Spectators spent the next few days waving bog rolls as he rode past. I'm still surprised that the eventual Giro winner never got offered a sponsorship deal with a toilet roll company.

Tom wasn't the first rider – and certainly won't be the last – to find himself with this kind of problem. It's a wonder that the French team FDJ used to insist on making their riders wear white shorts, which hide nothing. You'd think they would learn after a junior ended up on a lone breakaway that was completely unexpected. He had a dicky tummy but there were no team helpers to clean him up at the finish, so he ended up on the podium with badly stained shorts. The presentation team on the podium gave him a very wide berth.

Then Arnaud Démare (also riding for FDJ – is it something to do with the French diet?) pulled over by a camper van on a mountain stage of the Tour de France. He practically tore the door off its hinges and pushed his way past the owner, demanding to use the toilet.

Sean Kelly remarked to me, off air, 'Ah yes, he's got a dose of the scutters.'

'The scutters?'

'Yes. The scutters.'

Back live on air I said casually, 'Well, it seems that Arnaud Démare has had a dose of the, um… er… *scutters.*'

Sean's reaction seemed to me extreme: he mouthed a silent but dramatic *NOOOO!* and began shaking his head and waving his hands around. I carried on until the next ad break, when I turned back to Sean and asked, 'What is the scutters?'

It turns out that, as Sean put it, 'It's one of the worst fecking things you can say in Ireland!'

He explained that *scutters* means the shits, but it's more that that. It is simply the coarsest description of the worst possible trouser movement you can imagine. It's only the Irish who fully understand the dark meaning of it.

Back in Ireland, all the viewers were howling with laughter at the fact that 'that eejit Kirby just said the word *scutters* on live TV. Bet it was Sean put him up to it.'

Sometimes, of course, it is the facilities themselves that fail. On the women's Tour of Qatar back in 2013, the organisers had provided precisely one, yes one, solitary portable toilet cabin. For the entire field. Naturally, down the road, riders began to stop to relieve themselves. Somebody important went ballistic.

There are police everywhere, but in the Middle East there are also the Religious Police. Nobody, even the regular police, messes with the Religious Police. They carry big sticks and a big attitude. Someone high up was *very* upset at word of women relieving themselves outdoors, albeit due to poor planning. Next day there was an edict on the noticeboard. 'All competitors in need of taking a natural break must do so with modesty and out of sight. Riders will seek a place of privacy or face expulsion.'

Expulsion? That's out of the country, not just out of the race! This was patently ridiculous. Qatar is flat. Pancakes look mountainous in comparison. To find a 'place of privacy', riders would have to ride off-road towards the horizon, which would take 20 minutes to be 'out of sight'. There are no bushes to crouch behind.

It's not just riders that have come a cropper due to official toilet placement, either. At one remote, mountaintop village finish during the 2014 Giro, it was a hell of a business squeezing all the production vehicles into the tiny square. Anyway, we were all finally sorted – with not a spare centimetre left after the trucks and other facilities were installed either side of the finish line. Then we were informed that 'somebody local' wanted to park his car.

Apparently, this somebody was someone who was not the sort of person to take no for an answer. Not, at any rate, in southern Italy.

After much consternation, it was deemed that the only place Mr Somebody could park his car was where two Portaloos had been stationed: right next to the transmission truck. Clearly Mr Somebody wasn't going to walk anywhere, maybe due to fear of assassination or perhaps just because he couldn't be arsed. Fearing recriminations, the logistics guys set about making it possible.

The only thing they could move were the Portaloos. A cherry picker pitched up and set about lifting them up. Once the hooks were in place, the loos were raised. It was then that we began to hear the manic screaming. The crane operator, however, couldn't hear anything thanks to the noisy diesel engine. As the twinset of bogs was raised about 3–4m (12ft) off the ground, the door of one stall was flung open and a man stood, trousers down, clinging on to the door frame as a bowl of blue poo-soup slopped out all over his ankles. Happy days.

'IT'S ALL VERY WELL TAKING A BIG CHUNK, BUT YOU'VE GOT TO SWALLOW IT.'

10
ATTENTION SEEKERS!

What is it in the human psyche that makes us seek notoriety? And how is this to be achieved in the absence of luck or talent? Often this doesn't make for a dignified spectacle, especially when it comes to cycling. And so it is that we find Kevin the greengrocer from Bideford dressed in a lime green mankini running alongside elite athletes and emphasising the silky smooth legs of our heroes by displaying a pair of jiggling hirsute buttocks. He might be having fun. And at first he did raise a smile. But Kevin is not alone. The acid green mankini has been seen many times. Now even the addition of a ginger wig does not make it special. After many such visions, up many a mountain, this is a sight that has become bloody irritating.

There aren't any other major sports in the world where the spectator can get so close to their heroes. Cycling's arenas are the open roads that snake their way up alpine mountains and through everyday public streets. We have no need of Wembleys, Camp Nous and Maracanãs: we have the world to play with. Access to this world is free. There are no tickets. You only have to turn up with your trestle table and fold-up chair and 'Robert est ton oncle', you're in the thick of it. Up close and personal. There is nothing like this sort of access in any other sport. This is a cycling fan's privilege. Everyone is within touching distance of the superstars of the sport. And the unwritten contract that allows this to remain the case is that nobody is supposed to touch the competitors or affect the racing. Sadly, some of the fans are starting to get a bit too involved in the action itself. This is a problem.

The show-offs turn up in their myriad forms. And while I'm not a fan of CRS-style policing, I have a smidgen of sympathy for them when it comes to dealing with these idiots. I have to confess there have been some off-mike moments when we shout out in sheer joy as an outrunner in a dinosaur suit is run over by a police motorcycle. 'Oooh, I hope that hurts. . .'

When spectators start to have a negative influence on what happens in the race, then things have gone seriously wrong. Sure, there are the careless and accidental incidents such as untethered dogs bringing riders down. Handlebars getting caught in spectators' bags or camera straps. I can almost accept this as a product of the mass participation that makes cycling so great. But deliberate interference? No.

There are various forms of interference that I call out on air. You may have heard, 'Get out of the way you *idiot*,' or such like. Occasionally I'll go into detail about how the morons are harming the race. This is a genuine concern for the health and well-being of the riders. The perfect example of this is the havoc played out by those I call the Flare Boys.

What on earth is the idea – other than to create a spectacle with the instigator centre stage on his bit of turf along the course? What is it that motivates a 'fan' to take a powder flare along to a cycling event? They have been banned in many sports. You can be arrested at a football game for setting off such a smoke bomb. But not in cycling, where the governing body, the Union Cycliste Internationale (UCI), has failed to act.

The impact of phosphoric smoke pulled deep into the billowing lungs of a climbing cyclist is simply dangerous. I know I sound like an angry headmaster: 'What are they thinking? Morons!' But, I mean, how does their morning start off?

'I'm off to the cycling, love!'

'OK, honey, don't forget your powder flares!'

This on-air exchange with myself on the matter raised a few laughs on social media, but I was serious. Properly livid.

I was asked once if I thought I could have been held responsible for incitement. There was a fan running alongside the riders when another spectator lamped him, taking him clean out. It was a move once referred to in wrestling parlance as 'a forearm smash', and aimed squarely to the jaw. His legs went up in the air and he went bang to the ground, disappearing in his own smoke bomb. My thoughts remain my own on this, but I was seen to smirk.

Dutch Corner on Alpe d'Huez is perhaps a distillation of the extraordinary. Even driving through in a car you can hardly breathe from all the orange flares being deployed there. Maybe their name, Distress Flares, is apt . . . but it is the rider in distress. They're breathing so deeply on these peaks, desperately trying to oxygenate their blood, and they really don't need coloured smoke microparticles sucked into the depths of their lungs. It's an extreme irritant, and riders like Chris Froome who have a history of respiratory problems must actually hold their breath when they're going through particularly thick clouds of the stuff. Once a rider does that, especially when they're at their absolute max going up a mountain, the knock-on effect is huge.

So when I see some idiot setting off a distress flare next to the peloton, I go nuts. I think they should be banned and I say so on a regular basis on air. To what effect? Well, thankfully, at the 105th Tour de France, someone took note. I'm not saying I have the ear of Christian Prudhomme, the Race

Director, but he was once a Eurosport employee and I know he listens in. Anyway, a ban on flares would have required a change in the law in France. Instead, with just under a week left of the 2018 race, a request was issued to the local police along the remainder of the route, and this was accepted by the local prefectures.

Basically, in France if a police officer believes you to be a public nuisance – for example, playing music too loud, partying too late, etc – he can issue a desist order. If you ignore this, you can be arrested. The deployment of flares was added to the local lists of antisocial behaviour for the duration of the remaining race route. It was a clever way to deal with a situation that was getting out of hand; this had been a particularly smoky race.

Absolutely no more smoke was seen during the final six days on the Tour. I declared it 'the end of the moronathon'. I like to think I did my bit.

It remains to be seen if other races will adopt the same attitude towards flares – or, indeed, if the sport will insist on race organisers banning them. It may happen, but visit any number of cycling web pages and you'll see many pictures including flare smoke. It's fair to say that smoke billowing around a mountaintop does produce some fantastically dramatic pictures. The internet and the media is full of this stuff – and it makes great copy. On TV it begs a 'super-slo-mo' call from the director, particularly at the Giro d'Italia. But it is bonkers.

'ON PAPER DUMOULIN SHOULD WIN. BUT PAPER IS HIGHLY FLAMMABLE.'

MANKINI MAN COMES UP TRUMPS!

Every dog has his day, and for one mankini-clad peloton hound this day duly came: he landed the biggest, juiciest bone you can imagine.

On the Giro was a fan running alongside the riders in his underpants when one of the Nippo–Vini Fantini team punctured just next to where this guy was taking a breather from his near-naked exertions. The rider leapt off his dayglo yellow bike and turned to his team car for a replacement. The mechanic duly arrived and got a spare bike off the roof of the support car. Meanwhile, the very helpful Mankini Man held the original punctured bike at the side of the road; he didn't want to lay down such a beautiful and expensive bike on the ground. The rider was now on his spare bike, got the shove off from the mechanic and duly headed up the mountain, closely followed by the team car. But they'd forgotten about the first bike, held by Mankini Man! Our friend cried out and started trying to chase after them, waving and shouting, wheeling along this extraordinarily expensive, state-of-the-art, fully carbon racing machine. Dan Lloyd and myself were royally amused at the sight of it, battling our chuckles to carry on calling the race. But the story didn't end there.

At the end of the day, the mechanic counted up the bikes and realised that he'd left one behind. The pictures were all over the evening news. But the bike was nowhere to be found. The next day Nippo–Vini Fantini, who were being described as fools by all the reports, opted for the nuclear option. They made a formal complaint to the police. This didn't go down well.

To be fair, Nippo–Vini Fantini died as a team shortly after, so it was not as if they were awash with cash. A bike of this kind, depending on spec, can be around the €12,000 mark. That's a lot of money. Nonetheless, the general feeling among the public was that the scenario was a bit like catching a ball at a baseball game: the prize should stay with the catcher. A magistrate agreed and the edict was made that the fan had not stolen the bike but had indeed been gifted the prize – which he had, after all, tried to return. *Result!*

It warmed the heart: Mankini Man rode home a winner.

SKIPPY THE BUSHWHACKEROO

'Ohhhhh shit. It's Skippy. *Let's get outta here!*'

There are many obstacles to the smooth passing of a day. Some you can't avoid – like traffic jams or security checks. Others you can avoid with skill and good planning. But the biggest, and just about avoidable, barrier to a happy day is a bloke called Skippy. He's probably already borrowed this book off someone. Hi, Skippy!!

Skippy McCarthy has what I assume is a foxhole somewhere in Vienna, Austria. He's rumoured to have a place in Oz too, though many say he's actually a Brit. But Skippy is the ultimate cyclo-groupie, spending as little as possible in order to maximise his time following the Tour. Thus he has a tendency to try to get whatever he can from anyone connected with cycling. Clothes, food, accommodation, transport – anything. Light a barbecue, and you'll have a guest.

He often asks teams: 'Just a bidon, mate. . . Can I grab a shower? . . . Any ripped kit? . . . I've got a puncture. Help us out, mate.'

'Did I mention Kangaroo Reserve Preserve? We're selling jam to help orphan joeys! Ooh, is that egg going to waste?'

Skippy can be a real nuisance and on a long hot Tour, most of which he rides, he does get a bit whiffy. So why don't we just tell him to piss off? Well, firstly, he's a big bloke. Skinny but big. At the Tirreno Adriatico in 2014 I heard, 'Caaaaaaarlton… Over here, mate!!! *Caaaaaaarlton!*'

It was the first time I'd been tagged. I turned to walk over as Dan Lloyd walked on. I was a lamb to the slaughter. Thankfully I'm more mutton-like and not so tender.

'Hello. What's up?'

Skippy held out his hand. Before I could think, I responded politely and was shaking it. Big mistake! My hand was now firmly clamped in his big paw. I was trapped.

Skippy: 'All's good, mate! Where ya stayin'?'

'With Dan Lloyd.' I turned and pointed with my spare hand. Dan was leaning against a wall with one shoulder at an angle, arms folded. He was about 80m (260ft) away. He looked at me over his sunglasses, which sat halfway down his nose, like a teacher staring down a naughty kid. He shook his head very slowly to deliver the warning. He then pushed his specs back into place and looked away in a *Get on with it* kind of way. Get on with telling Skippy to piss off. I got the message.

'Gotta go. Sorry!' Using my other hand, I pushed against his forearm and pulled my hand clear.

Skippy wasn't happy: 'Look, I'm here for the Keep the Koala campaign, mate. Where are you staying? I need to talk to you about the campaign.'

I'm already off at a brisk pace, like an Olympic walker.

Skippy loses it: 'WHERE YA F--KIN' STAYIN', EURO-F--KIN'-SPORT . . . WHERE ARE YA? . . . THINK OF THE KOALAS!!!'

To his credit, Skippy fundraises for a myriad of causes. For a couple of seasons he was a mobile billboard for Kids With Cancer Foundation Australia. Lately he's switched to the Stop Killing Cyclists 'safe passing distance' initiative. He carries card-backed posters of these worthy campaigns and has thus managed to get himself photographed with an arm around the shoulders of the likes of Alberto Contador.

'Hi, mate, riding for Kids With Cancer. Can I borrow your room for a mo? Just a shower, mate. It's for the kids, after all. Eh, mate?'

This is the kind of line you fall for just once. On his first Tour, a kindly David Harmon handed Skippy his room key. About two hours later and after much knocking, David had to get the hotel staff to let him in. There he found Skippy fast asleep in bed, with all his washing hanging wet around the room.

Harmon: 'Skippy, you're in my bed!'

Skippy, stirring: 'No worries, mate, we can split it. You take the mattress and I'll use the base.'

Harmon: 'Er . . .'

Skippy: 'Hey, it's for Kids With Cancer, mate!'

An uncomfortable night ensued. Next morning, Skippy is in the shower calling out: 'Where are we staying tonight, David?'

Harmon: 'I'll just check. Give me a mo...'

A hasty escape plan saw Kelly and Harmon slipping away quietly as Skippy towelled down. He probably heard the tyres screeching away through the open window.

But the boys were not quite in the clear.

After the day's broadcast, they headed towards the open highway. As they reached the tollbooths, there was Skippy, waiting on the other side of the barriers . . . for them!

Kelly was driving. 'Ohhhh shite, he's seen us!!!'

Screaming 'Eurosport . . . Heeeey, Euuuuuuro-f--kin-spoooooort!!!', Skippy was heading their way, dodging the cars being released from the tollbooths. Still behind the barrier, Kelly took the ticket in a panic and hit the accelerator. One of Skippy's paws slammed on the roof.

'Give us a f--kin' lift, you bastards! Don't you care about KIDS WITH CANCER??!!!' he screamed at the departing Skoda Estate.

They were gone. And a lesson was learned by David.

'Never speak to that eejit again. Understand?' said Kelly.

David just nodded in shock. He'd been Skippied.

'HE FLIES UP HILLS EXACTLY AS BRICKS DON'T.'

11
PROTESTERS

If you're into the Rolling Stones, you'll know that, for Jumpin' Jack Flash, life is a gas, gas, gas. But if you're into rolling hay bales on to the Tour de France route, then be prepared for the flash of stun grenades and plenty of gas, gas, gas as well. This is the latest round of the French way of dealing with disputes. Protest first as a starting point . . . then talk. It's sort of the opposite to the British way. In France they get the percussive bit over with early on, then pick up the pieces. I was told by a colleague that this method defines the ground rules early on and can end with a glass of wine and a handshake – albeit between bandaged hands. The Brits go the other way with disputes: all nicey, nicey at first. Slowly things smoulder. A few scuffles, then arbitration. Nobody knows what the baseline standpoint is until the very last. Drags on for ages, everyone miffed.

I do see the point in the French revolutionary way. After all, it served them well in the past. But sadly it's a method that doesn't mix with cycling. If a local disgruntled workforce decides to get the bale rolling, so to speak, it can prove disastrous. This happened on Stage 16 of the 2018 Tour de France.

The run to Bagnères-de-Luchon was 218km (135 miles) long and was meant to be tough. It came after the second rest day and involved five climbs, getting progressively harder. There were two Category 1s at the end and a downhill run to the line. It was a day made for a breakaway. The teams knew this and so it took a lot of time before the group established itself up the road. Finally, after an hour of many attempted formations, 41 riders pulled clear of the main challengers for the title and headed up the road. This group was an impressive fighting force and was destined to contain the stage winner. The challengers would have their own battle behind this gang of breakers. And so it was that after a very feisty start to the day we thought we'd settled into a calm period. Oh no.

En route a very cleverly planned ambush was being implemented. A tower of round hay bales had been stacked close to the race route. On top of these were the protesters, disguised as happy race fans. They were dancing and shouting as one might expect. Advance security had indeed been fooled and so much of the police force guarding the route had passed by, along with the advanced organisation vehicles. Then, just as the riders were approaching, the protesters went into action. Tractors moved in and the bales were pushed into the road. Police arrived just ahead of the riders and officers were seen putting themselves in front of charging machines carrying bale spikes that threatened life and limb. Tear gas was deployed.

The day was a still one. It felt pre-stormy. This was bad news for the riders who, of course, came to a halt. As the protesters wrestled with the now significant police presence, the billowing gas duly wafted gently over the riders. They stood astride their bikes with tears running down their cheeks. The race was, of course, neutralised. Medical teams ran out of eyewash; riders complained of breathing troubles. For 30 minutes we waited until everyone was well enough to go on.

Usually in such circumstances, there is a kind of accord called by the race organisation. Protesters threatening to block the road are asked to stand at one side and display their banners spelling out their grievances. These are then shown on television – and everyone is happy. This time, there was absolutely no accord. The protesters were castigated and even arrested. Their message went undelivered.

The riders responded passively. Probably, I suppose you could say, because they had been gassed. More likely, it is the understanding that the race security is much more effective these days and it's best to leave this to the professionals. This wasn't always the case.

In the 1984 edition of the Paris–Nice, Bernard Hinault had made a spectacular attack off the Col de l'Espigoulier. He and about 20 riders had broken clear of Hinault's main rival, Robert Millar, who began the day as leader. All was going well for the French star until some protesting shipyard workers decided to block the road ahead. They stood there in donkey jackets, black wool with a plastic panel over the shoulders offering modest protection against the steady drizzle. There was a high quota of berets, moustaches and Gauloises on display. It looked very French. It was also a bit half-arsed in terms of organisation. They shuffled into position looking almost embarrassed as they mumbled their protest chants into the mist of a cold wet mid-March afternoon. Well, things were about to heat up.

Down the road the protesters saw Hinault. This was their moment. The chants grew louder and more committed. Sadly for them, so was Hinault. Fully. Instead of slowing down, Hinault accelerated. He was livid. These protesters could cost him the lead! Faster and faster, Hinault drove his bike on towards the human barricade. The protesters held their ground, but the chanting stopped. Insults flew towards Hinault, then silence – just for a split second, you understand, as everyone standing in the road realised there was about to be an accident. Hinault smashed into the group, sending the workers scattering. Game over? Oh no! Hinault was already off his bike, sending his swinging fists into moustachioed faces. They couldn't believe it. Stunned, the workers took the blows from this madman. Who was mad as hell. Before the men with broken cigarettes between their bloody lips could return the blows, the organisers pulled The Badger off his quarry. Hinault had just written another page of his impressive history. The Badger is a notoriously grumpy animal. Magnificent.

So listen! If you want to continue enjoying your cycling live at a roadside near you, there are a few things we need to get sorted. Keep your protests off the road. Don't bring flares. Don't drape flags over your heroes, shouting 'Olé': it can tangle with a bike's mechanics and cause a crash. Don't splash riders with water: it can hamper vision. Don't 'help' by pushing them uphill: it breaks a climber's rhythm. Don't bare your arse. And don't wear outfits that can trip you up and bring down a rider.

One of the greatest characteristics of cycling is that anyone can just turn up at the side of the road and enjoy it for free. If this is to continue, we need mutual respect between spectators and riders. If you are one of the roadside fools, then be certain I will be calling you out for it. You might of course think this a bonus if notoriety is all you are after.

To the real fans, I say that when your heroes pass by, do please feel entirely free to go suitably nuts in all the excitement. I certainly do.

'THE PENDULUM HAS SWUNG, AS THEY SAY IN COMMENTATING. TO BE FAIR, CLOCKMAKERS USE THE TERM AS WELL.'

12
SLOW DAY

Padding and filler. Generally used to enhance something for reasons of aesthetics or necessity. But let's consider the period during many a transition or sprint stage that needs a bit of help from a commentator to keep things interesting. It's time to ponder . . . nothing . . . and work out how to bridge it.

It's 11.10 a.m. and Tour de France supremo Christian Prudhomme has just popped his head out of his sunroof to prove that no matter how much money you have, hair transplants remain a game played by those with less self-confidence. So, like HRH Prince William, a man truly at peace with his fallow areas, Christian emerges from the, usually red, Race Director's car and flaps his outstretched arms like an albatross – slowly. This brings everyone to order. Before we go racing, all those wearing the various classification leaders' jerseys have posed at the front for the cameras. Their toil will usually come much further down the road. So, with TV photo ops done, the bigger names drift away as the band of hopeful escapee brothers prepare themselves to do the job for which, at breakfast, they have been chosen by their Directeur Sportif:

'Get your skinny arse into the break and show off the team jersey which you are being paid to wear. See Gianni Savio for your wages.'

And they're off! Sometimes the break goes clear immediately. Meanwhile, everyone else does the decent thing and promptly takes a comfort break. This is going to be a *long* day.

Oh dear.

THE EASIEST JOB IN THE WORLD?

What now? As a commentator, it is my job to pass comment. Let's hope there's something to say because this fairly nondescript day will end in around five hours with a sprint. Sure, it will be remembered for the drama of the approach. The break will get caught at around 18km (11 miles) to go and a frantic finale will make the highlights show. So . . . what to do for the remaining four and a half hours?

There is only so much news, so much tech or rider palmarès to go through before those commentators who work 'from the page' run out of material. A stage guided by a research monkey will be as dry as a cracker. When all material has gone, they finally default to interviewing the colour commentator, usually an ex-pro. This is known in the trade as 'passing the mike' or indeed 'taking the mike'. And so it all starts to *draaaaag*. It's porridge. Time, then, for a scoop of Tutti-Frutti. Some tasty colour.

ENCYCLOPAEDIA CARLTONICA

11.25 a.m. The peloton has settled into the relative amble of a mass tap. This is not a protest. The break has formed and gone. It suits everyone. They might be allowed a gap of, say, 11 minutes' temptation time on the peloton, just so the underdogs believe there's a chance of survival. Everyone back in the pack is happy. It's a day for the quick men so, for everyone else, it's simply a task of getting through the stage and letting the rockets loose at the end. No panic yet. And no action until the end.

Around now, the viewer begins to be shown the familiar magnificence of France. The director is a guy called Jammo, short for Jean Maurice. He's been doing this since his hair was black. His considerable locks are now white as snow, just like his reputation. He is a genius. Jammo, or Monsieur Confiture as he's known among the Brits, starts to paint the day with sumptuous shots. Some are live and some 'in the can'. As he weaves his magical interludes away from the gently cruising riders, we get reminded why this is the greatest theatre for a bike race on the planet. France is simply gorgeous. Even when it's dodgy, like Brest or Lens, it's still gorgeous.

But pictures are not enough. Hours of mountains, beaches, lakes, chateaux, vineyards, notable landmarks and so on, they need a guide. This is when commentators really earn their crust. Anyone can call a dramatic mountain finish with the field spread out in a battle of attrition to the top. But this is not that day. A Mogadon day needs waking up. Hello!?

Luckily, I have a memory that's a lexicon of facts, figures, images and stories that I've built up over the years. How extensive this library is, I have no idea. You see, I don't ever throw away a memory. Everything is in there. I am always reminding people of what they have done.

'How the hell do you remember that?' they say.

'Well, I have no idea to be honest. But I never forget a thing.'

That's not to say my memories are in any kind of order. There is no filing system. It's an emporium in there and it's easy to open a drawer that has been closed for decades. Up pops a thought or a tale that even I am happily surprised to find. And it could be anything. The slightest trigger will set me off. Honestly, even when I'm not broadcasting I'm often asked: 'What are you smiling at?' I'm simply busy chuckling to myself as another random page of this crazy life's diary is recovered for my own amusement. It's fun to go for a rummage around in there. I do it all the time. And sometimes, particularly on quiet days, I take the audience with me. And so it is that the commentary can become a bit random as the *Encyclopaedia Carltonica* is opened up.

It's an absolute mishmash of information, from crop rotation and farming methods to roof tile manufacturing, both ancient and modern, in south-west France. Grape varieties, sausage production, the healthy properties of zinc worktops – all this and more alongside anthropological studies of South Pacific islanders and an extensive knowledge of cloud formations and the prevailing winds of the Mediterranean. It can be medicinal, commercial, poetic, historic – and sometimes all of these things.

'Brian, did you know that the monks who produce the Benedictine Liqueur never actually get to taste it? And that their biggest market as measured per head of population is actually Hartlepool? A Hot Benny has been hugely popular there since troops returning from the First World War, who had been billeted in the monastery, came home with the stuff. Pubs add warm water to it to make a winter hot toddy.'

To which Brian Smith, twice British Champion, will simply say, 'Er, no. I didn't know that', in his soft Paisley accent.

There are, of course, guides to help out the less anecdotally loaded. Such lexicons will tell you that: 'The thimble of Belafonte is the smallest to be found in the Loire valley.' This is small beans. While one commentator might pitch for this as a filler, I will be busy regaling the viewer with the rudiments of manufacturing gaufrettes as we pass a biscuit factory.

'I drove a forklift there as a summer job back in the mid 1970s. I really did, Biscuiterie Rouger in La-Haye-du-Puits. Bernard Hinault was on the telly in the canteen. Naturally. My pal, Mark, ordered whelks and asked me for advice on a rather black one he'd just curled out of its shell. I said I had no idea but added that they are usually green. With a ho-hum shrug, he went for it and ended up in hospital . . . Er, you still with us, Sean?'

'IT'S LIKE BRINGING A CATAPULT TO A NUCLEAR WAR.'

A TOUGH NIGHT AT A CYCLING CLUB

As a result of my verbal meanderings, I've gained myself a bit of a reputation as something of a wanderer during races. So I was more than a little surprised when I was approached at the end of a charity dinner by someone from Kenton Road Cycling Club. They were celebrating their 75th anniversary, and there was a founder member in the audience. He was 89. Up he wandered. There was I thinking that my hosting of the night's raffle was in for a compliment. But no.

'Do you know what annoys me about your sort?' he said. 'You commentators. We pass by all these chateaux and all this wonderful landscape and scenery and you never mention them.'

'Are you an ITV viewer?' I asked him.

'Yes.'

'In that case, we've got nothing to say to each other. Because that's my stock in trade. I am famous for going off-piste. If I did it any more, I'd be a tourist guide.'

He wouldn't let go: 'You see, there is so much to talk about regarding the scenery and so on.'

'I KNOW THERE IS,' I said, my volume rising slightly as I made allowance for what I assumed must be deafness rather than simple bloody-mindedness. 'THAT'S WHAT I DO, YOU SEE. YOU ARE CLEARLY WATCHING SOMEONE ELSE. DO YOU UNDERSTAND?'

'Well it's just not good enough . . .' Etc, etc.

A friend of mine once decided to make a documentary featuring people over 100 years old. He said it was so depressing. Rather than offering up jolly reminiscences of a long life, they were all simply the most miserable curmudgeons he could imagine. Basically, they complained about everything. Nothing in their lives was either good enough or as good as it used to be. Well, wake up, Grandad, there is more cycling on telly than there has ever been and my job is to keep it lively.

'IF YOU ARE WATCHING SOMEONE ELSE, I CAN TAKE NO RESPONSIBILITY,' I added. I think I then said 'git' under my breath.

'What did you just call me?'

Clearly his hearing worked just fine when it suited him.

'YOU ARE CLEARLY NOT WATCHING E – U – R – O – F – S – P – O – R – T.'

'There's no F in Eurosport!'

'PRECISELY! NO EFFING EUROSPORT, AND I SUGGEST YOU SUBSCRIBE.'

Time to go home.

THE MAN WITH THE GOLDEN MICROPHONE

If it's an action-packed day, especially a mountain stage, then our job becomes somewhat easier. That's because, believe it or not, we know what we're talking about. Well, most commentators do. Not all, though. And if one is prepared to wade in to a sport where the home audience is generally rather knowledgeable, then . . . oh dear!

I knew a certain Dutch commentator who claimed that he had once been awarded the highly coveted and, as far as I know, entirely fictional prize of The Golden Microphone for his supposedly excellent sports commentary in the Netherlands. Somehow he'd ended up at Eurosport and he was renowned for being the most appalling commentator – it didn't matter what it was, from football or tennis to speed skating or beach volleyball, he was hopeless. Why was he there? Schmooze. He was an amazing schmoozer. He wined and dined at the finest restaurants and his guests were the main men at the top of the organisation. He was even one of the select few who sailed the company yacht. Yes, that's right. The yacht. Eurosport was owned largely by TF1, the equivalent of ITV in the UK. France being an apparently proletarian republic and TF1 surviving with a good deal of public help, everything within the organisation was to be shared equally. Equally among those who knew, obviously. This yacht was virtually Top Secret. There was no application process for access to enjoy its decks, either bobbing in Nice harbour or out at sea. No, this was a secret shared among the elite. And our friend was one of those.

One sport after another fell by the wayside as producers came to realise that the new boy was not up to scratch in any way save for bravado, gold teeth (of which he had plenty), and a rather liquorice voice that had got him through the door in the first place.

One day it was the turn of cycling to welcome our friend to the microphone. And what a day it was. The Queen stage – the hardest, most demanding stage of the tour and therefore the most prestigious. The regular commentator was down after a dodgy andouillette for lunch out on the course. This meant that our friend would voice the day remotely, from the Paris hub studio.

For what follows, let's call our friend GM, in honour of his award.

The conversation went something like this:

'GM, do you know anything about cycling? We're desperate for a commentator on today's big Tour de France stage, can you do it?'

'Of course I can. I didn't win the Golden Microphone for nothing, you know.'

'Okay. So it's the Queen stage, the most important of the whole Tour de France. You obviously know that this is the big one, the decider. Now, are you sure you can get up to speed with this iconic day and all the history attached? Do you understand how important this is?'

'The Queen stage. Well, yes, of course that's not a problem. Just leave it to me. I'll be absolutely fine. I am, after all, the winner of the Golden Microphone.'

If Mont Ventoux did get mentioned, it was perhaps lost in the panic. But surely everyone knew what was to come; GM was as confident as ever. And so the day began.

To be fair, GM acquitted himself satisfactorily for the first few uneventful opening parts of the stage. As they approached Mont Ventoux, even he was able to pick up on the rising tension and stress within the peloton as riders vied for a good place at the front of the pack. The mighty climb loomed over them and they began to tackle the lower slopes that are hemmed in by trees before it opens up into the famous lunar landscape that is the Bald Mountain.

Just below the tree line on Ventoux, before you get to the barren, brutal, desolate and windswept flanks of this terrible mountain, is Chalet Reynard. It's here that you can find a road sign telling riders and drivers alike whether the pass is open or not. This road often becomes blocked by snowdrifts in winter and high winds in springtime, but being the height of summer, it was of course open. 'Col Ouvert' said the helpful sign, which was picked up by the TV camera on the back of the motorbike as it chased the pack upwards.

GM's commentary went something like this:

'So here we are. The riders approach this iconic, famous climb. This is the big one, folks, the one we've all been waiting for. The mountain that defines the Tour de France. So much history. Just think of all the famous battles that have been fought on this monstrous mountain. It is, of course, that most epic of all mountains, the Col Ouvert.'

I remember the reaction of the producer of the day. It was Patrick Chasse, a man who remains a big noise in the French cycling world. He was watching the screen and even though he didn't speak Dutch he had a sense of what had just been uttered.

'What did that monkey just say?' he asked Jurriaan Van Wessem, an equally renowned journalist from the world of football.

'I believe he just referred to the world-famous Col Ouvert,' he said with a smirk.

'In – croy – fooking – able!' was Patrick's rather entertaining Franglais take on the matter. Our friend GM did not do cycling again.

'MY BRAIN IS LIKE A BOX OF FROGS ON ACID.'

LAZY MONKS

No matter how dramatic a mountaintop finish turns out to be, it is usually a story that tells itself. The drama unfolds slowly, with the riders clearly visible and in small numbers. Their dogged battle is a chance for a commentator to call it home comfortably. This is a lily that needs no gilding. So if you want to measure the value of a commentator, then listen to a boring day: a transitional stage. One where nothing at all happens for hours on end. That is where a good commentator carries the day. Like a sherpa, often without much credit, a good commentator gets you to the line in good spirits, having carried you there despite the tedium.

On quiet days, some filler subjects crop up more than others. Usually things that annoy me get a lot of time. I'm not given to overt grumpiness for the sake of it, but certain things really rile me and on a quiet day they get on air. One of the stalwart subjects is Lazy Monks. There are a lot of them about.

Monte Cassino is a rocky hill about 130km (80 miles) south-east of Rome and was the site where Benedict of Nursia established his first monastery around the year 529. This sanctuary was the site of the horrific and bloody Battle of Monte Cassino in 1944, when it was destroyed by Allied bombing in an attempt to dislodge the German forces who were dug in to the impressively thick walls. The damage was extensive and the fighting was intense. What remained after the battle was a sad reflection of what had been before. As a result, a World Heritage Fund was established to make good what had been destroyed. Decades later the transformation is amazing, so I am told. For despite having visited the venerable building on the mount, I have not seen inside it.

On a day when the cycling world came by, it was – as usual for us – shut. It may well have said: 'Gates closed. Go away.' I find this simply infuriating, particularly when the world has paid such enormous sums to these institutions, either to maintain them or indeed rebuild them. Such places are only open to the chosen. Sadly, this righteous list does not include cycle fans. They don't want squeaky sport shoes going round their basilicas.

So there I am, fuming on air, as we sat at the finish line just 30m (100ft) or so from the locked gates of the monastery. On what was a quiet day I had time to rant and knew it would not be long before the on-site producer from RCS Sport, the organisers of the Giro, would come to visit me. He calls me Cialtrone. It's not affectionate.

'Cialtrone, it is time to stop these critical words.'

Meet Roberto Nitti, a nervous man in a high stress job that he does very well. He can be quick to anger and paces around the compound in a festering, beady-eye kind of way. *Cialtrone*, by the way, means 'slob' in Italian. I like the joke.

During a break, Francesco, one of the rather excessively suave Italian commentators from Rai Uno, slides an arm over my shoulders. It's like being introduced to a pet python. With this weight on my shoulders, I dare not move as his tobacco-dipped voice whispers some advice.

'Carlton, Carlton,' he said. 'You have to play the game.'

'What?'

'You phone beforehand,' he said. 'You go and interview the Abbot. And then you have a private tour.'

Well, perhaps the lockout was a blessing in disguise because it gave me at least 20 minutes of transmission time while I stuck the boot in. Now, though, whenever I see gates to a monastery I simply have to stop the car and get someone to take a photo of me trying to force them open. Lazy monks. Can't stand 'em!

BAROLO: NO BARREL O' LAUGHS

I love it when the Giro passes through some of the smaller, insignificant villages and towns where the locals really celebrate the whole event. Often you can go to some of the poorest and most modest areas of Italy, and here the press corps will be treated like royalty. These areas are charming and unpretentious. They may well not have much, but they're determined to share what they do have with you. This might be a small bottle of wine as a gift or even a little book of local postcards. Lovely. They have usually put on some kind of catering, and a local dish will be top of the list. It's usually served up by kids from the local schools, who have the day off. Everyone is all smiles and the atmosphere is just perfect: low key and lovely. It's like a family gathering. Everyone is chatty, and we find out about them and a little bit about their area. Wonderful.

And then we have the likes of Barolo.

Barolo wine has, unjustly in my opinion, carved out a reputation for itself as one of the country's premier Italian reds, with its self-proclaimed rich and velvety texture. The vines are ancient and the area is full of old money. It is a *very* wealthy place.

There is not a dog turd in sight or a bus ticket blown through the street. The holy vines look like they've been not just pruned but manicured. You go past all these beautiful estates and villas where, for generations, these families have been very well off indeed, thank you very much. Even when the wars have washed through, the landed and branded could buy favours with a great big barrel of wine and remained untouched and impregnable. None of the good stuff ever got bombed. I see it as my job to chip away at these institutions.

When the Giro passed through Barolo, they provided absolutely nothing! This was in stark contrast to their poorer cousins further south. However, we the media are supposed to write about Barolo, broadcast about Barolo and take photographs of Barolo. For this, all they gave us was their reputation. What's more, they shunned the entire event. As if we were supposed to be grateful just being allowed to be there.

Barolo, one of the richest micro regions of Planet Earth, didn't even provide water for the press corps. And it was a hot day. The press were getting grumpy. There wasn't a coffee machine to be found.

There was even a wine tasting where – and this is where some press guys lost it – you were expected to pay! If you want to wind up a group of journalists, just make them pay for everything. Apparently their pumped-up, over-muscular, eat-only-with-aged-liver-or-well-hung-game plonk was too valuable to be given graciously and freely to those supposed to comment on it. Remarkable.

Then, when we were broadcasting the stage and at a crucial part of the race, the cameras cut away and dwelled on, for some time, a helicopter shot of a vast and notable Barolo wine estate. To me, this whiffed of a prior arrangement, airtime considered a fair swap by the TV direction crew in return for some of the local produce. There were big close-up shots of the winemaker's signs, giving it global publicity and free advertising. My comment on air was, 'I guarantee you that someone's going to be sending a transit van round to be filled up with wine from that estate because there's no reason whatsoever for it to be on your screens while so much is happening in the race.' I got my arse kicked all round the TV compound for that comment – I suspect because it was true.

A quick note to my friends in Barolo: technology has caught up with you guys. There are obviously many, many wine shops over in the UK. On average, Barolo can be found 40 per cent cheaper in the United Kingdom. I could go to Majestic Wine round the corner from my home and get exactly the same bottle for significantly less without having to lug it around Italy for a few weeks.

So there you have another 20 minutes killed or crafted – depending on your opinion of what I do. You could call it filler. I call it fun! OK, grumpy fun, with a score settled.

But, other than engaging in knocking down institutions and pillars of the hierarchy, I always find that a bit of idle chat about Sean Kelly's dinner choices the night before or what drinks sent me and Dan Lloyd under the table make for a good bit of banter.

Then there's so much news from the teams that you pick up when you're on site – you find out a lot. There's no excuse for not being entertaining when not much is going on. That's part of the job. If it sounds easy, then you're doing it well.

I often compare commentary to that nightmare where you're walking around town with no clothes on. On occasion, you find yourself completely exposed and your job is to find a hiding place, bury the issue and keep the show on the road. We're like that old adage about a swan: all serene on the surface but going like the clappers underneath the surface. When I started my career in the BBC regions and then TV-am, I was told by both institutions that I was far too relaxed and laconic. That is indeed how I come across to some folk. I think it's a kind of self-preservation mechanism for when things start to get a bit hairy. Some animals pretend to be dead when they're in danger. I just chill out and crack a joke. I may appear to be cool and calm on the outside but I'm probably desperately tense and juggling for my life on the inside.

'KENNY DE KETELE IS AT A SIMMER AT THE MOMENT BUT HE'S READY TO BOIL OVER.'

13
FEED STATION

The physical demands for a rider on a Grand Tour are enormous. In fact, it's estimated that a rider will burn more than 6,000 calories a day, meaning that they are constantly trying to refuel their bodies with enough nutrition to make a very long journey over challenging terrain possible. Sure, the riders set off in the morning with gels in their pockets and full water bottles in the cages. And although these are replaced regularly, with the help of the poor sod who has been chosen to go back to the car for bottles, this is not enough to keep everyone going. So it is that race organisers are duty-bound to build a Feed Station into the riders' day. This zone is a challenging place. Every rider must first find his 'swanny', or soigneur, the team member whose role is to locate themselves evenly along the road while plaintively calling out squad names into the wind. This is no easy task: they have to hold quite a considerable weight high enough in the air to allow the rider to grab the long-handled goody bag safely.

This whole delivery business is fraught with danger. As the swannies' arms, along with their smiles, begin to tire, the bag drops from its early enthusiastic height to what can be a challenging altitude for the rapidly approaching rider. If the top of the sack handles drop from being held proud in the air to around the chest height of the holder, there will be trouble.

Grabbing a knapsack too high up the long handles causes 'bag swing'. This is a problem. The ideal place to catch a bag at, say, 25km/h (15mph) is close to the bag itself. The higher you are up the handles on collection, the further away you are from a perfect take. The bag becomes a pendulum, sometimes weighing a couple of kilos or more. This then swings violently behind the back of the rider, who then veers off line, losing control. A bag-swinging rider can easily collect others around him – and often does. No wonder, then, that feed zones are, at best, places of argumentative finger pointing and, at worst, crashes and injury. So, in more ways than one, riders need to take their feeding seriously, approaching the matter with both focus and skill.

TREATS!

The inquisitive and sharp-eyed among you will, I'm sure, have noticed that some of the items emerging from riders' knapsacks are far from the standard fare you might be tempted to buy off the shelves in the bike store. Forget hi-tech gels and bars; in the peloton, some extras inside the bags can be a bit freestyle, to say the least.

These occasional non-standard items might be there to satisfy the peculiar tastes of a star rider, or a treat designed to cheer up a flagging athlete – a candy bar, say, or a Coke. Other items are sometimes included simply to make riders laugh.

One former Dutch Champion tells of a rider in the gruppetto bursting out laughing on a particularly miserable day in Belgium after opening a sandwich that had been lovingly wrapped in a page from a porn magazine. Apparently this was started by an American team. The mirth spread as the page was handed around. It raised the spirits of a damp and grumpy band of brothers whose job of driving the peloton in the opening hours had been done. The porn habit soon spread to other teams and became a real diversion on long hard days, so to speak. Sadly, when this became an obsession for the riders, who would look forward to the rude stuff being handed out, the team managers stamped on it. The sight of riders zigzagging to get a look at the latest piece of filth was being caught by TV cameras. Not good for the sponsors.

JELLY, SPAM AND FIGS – A RECIPE FOR DISASTER

The whole sedentary lifestyle of commentating, coupled with plenty of rich French, Italian or Spanish food, tends to have a swelling effect on my body. And having the top-heavy physique of a rower doesn't exactly give me the classic svelte figure of a cyclist. To be frank, after a few weeks on a Grand Tour, any interview I might do with Chris Froome should carry a graphic tag: *The Stick and Ball Show.*

Rather than try to hide my mass, I tend just to badge it up. The Americans help out in this department significantly. Firstly, ads for cycle gear stateside sometimes offer the tempting headline: 'Look Like a Pro right up to XXXXXL'. That's five Xs, by the way. Pity the guy who needs six! I slip gently into just two. OK, three.

Couple this with some rather self-deprecating team names that look good on any end of the balloon scale right up to Goodyear Blimp. Indeed, Goodyear has just re-entered the cycling market after a break of 120 years. Surely this is just for me! Where's my complimentary kit?

Conveniently, there are a number of cycling teams whose name brings an acceptable irony to a tubby rider: I did consider the JellyBelly team, who have kindly graced the sport for some time. However, their kit, although great, lacked a certain uniqueness. Then I came across a SPAM jersey . . . in XXXL. Featuring a picture of a SPAM fritter burger front and back, with a mere suggestion of salad, the logo read: SPAM . . . CRAZY TASTY! This I had to have.

The enormous yellow and blue jersey was forced through my regular-sized letterbox by a huffing and puffing postman just before I departed for the Tour of Turkey.

My mate Brian Smith and I took our well-packed Vitus bikes to the airport, and hoped they would survive the journey to Istanbul. These had been kindly loaned us by Sean Kelly's An Post–Chain Reaction team. They didn't provide any clothing kit, so naturally I took my new pride and joy.

Turkey has some spectacular scenery. Its people are among the most welcoming in the world. Their food is amazing and the cycling is superb. Strange, then, that I managed to mash up all these wonderful elements into a near-unholy disaster.

On the day of a team time trial, we finished early, giving Brian and me a chance to get on the bikes and head inland away from the coast. Brian is a former professional rider who has competed in Grand Tours, not to mention the Olympic and Commonwealth Games, and he's clearly a much better and fitter cyclist than I could ever be. 'You going out in that?' said Bri in his Paisley burr. 'You're having a laugh!'

'Yeah, good, isn't it! Got it sent over from the States.'

And with that, off I set to get a margin on the man with thighs like granite-filled sandbags. Very quickly Bri cruised up alongside. Arriving smoothly and silently with threatening intent, like a sleek Zeppelin. We rode on for a while together with Bri looking at me and shaking his head gently as he issued the occasional 'Sheesh!' By now, I was also shaking my head, but from side to side as I tried to keep up with him.

Unsurprisingly, we ended up going our separate ways. He disappeared up a mountain, while I decided to take an easier route. It was still pretty hilly, but I was happy spinning along through the countryside and little villages. The road kicked up and naturally my pace slowed. Then, as I ploughed up through a village surrounded by fig groves, my troubles started.

What struck me was the way folk looked at me and stirred from their relaxed state, becoming tense. Men stood up and told their kids to go indoors. As I struggled up the modest incline in the heat of the late afternoon, one house called out to the next to warn neighbours of my approach. I was now being greeted by men and women at the edge of their land with hissing sounds and what were clearly insults. They were getting quite animated! I pushed on.

Out the other side of a village, the road I was on simply petered out into a dirt track that was too rough for my road bike. This, of course, meant I had to turn back. Oh dear.

I was about 200m (656ft) clear of the top of the village and down below me the road was filling with my friends. I stopped in a moment of would-be Clint Eastwood cool and cleaned my glasses as I pondered my fate through squinting eyes. I was going to have to go for it. Specs on and head down, I grabbed the bars like a track cyclist and braced myself. I could imagine the start gate at the velodrome about to release me. Everyone in the road below stopped too. As the dust around their feet struggled to settle in the orange twilight, there was a brief staredown. I tensed. In my head I heard the starter countdown: 'Booop, booop, booop, *beep*!' I was off.

As soon as I began my run, the crowd immediately started theirs.

I picked up pace quickly with some of the slickest gear changes I've ever done. Cool as a cucumber, I was about to be met with . . . figs. Lots of figs. A figgy blizzard indeed.

As I got within about 50m (165ft), I was going at around 60km/h (37mph) and I was looking good. But not for long.

The first rotten fig caught me on my collarbone and exploded up the right side of my face. The sweet jammy smell was a counterpoint to the verbal bile being issued my way. This was a cue to everyone to let loose. The crowd numbered no more than 40, but their hit rate was impressive. As my vision was gone in seconds thanks to three headshots, I naturally slowed dramatically. I can report that clincher brakes struggle with fig jam. Coming to a juddering halt, I pulled off my specs. Thankfully, the mood had changed and everyone was now laughing uproariously. I smiled just in time to see a kid on his dad's shoulders tip a boxful of purple fruit grenades over me. I waddled through them. Clipped in and rode away to the sound of an entire village in wild celebration.

Ten minutes down the road, Brian pulled up alongside me. 'What the f--k happened to you?'

Waving a couple of wasps away, I told him. '. . . and they just f--kin' pelted me! For no good reason whatsoever!'

'It's a bloody Muslim country, idiot. Spam is a pork product, you dickhead.'

'Ah! Let's get the hell out of here.'

FOOD FIGHTS

Racing is about power and delivery.

In my view, Formula 1 racing is largely about the car. In cycling, it's about the man. Sure, the bike comes into the equation, but it's the man numbers that matter.

A good engine and aero package is vital. In motorsport, this is about light alloy power units and bodywork. In cycling, it is the rider himself who provides these elements. Now, as we all know, if you get the fuelling wrong for any engine, it's likely to go pop! Let's ponder this.

A rider struggles to get 6,000 calories into his body to cope with the physical torment of a regular racing day. Such are the demands of cycling for four hours and more at a pace that, even in cruise mode, would see off even the best club riders after 20 minutes. Fuelling such a feat of endurance takes dedication to ingestion. And sometimes indigestion.

Getting prepped wrong brings on the knock, where energy levels collapse – as do, sometimes, the riders themselves. This physical demise can happen with dramatic speed, and even the best riders in the world can suddenly come close to fainting and begin weaving across the road. As soon as these earliest signs present themselves, there is not much time to act. The body can short-circuit without the power derived from food and its internal resources. Get your feed wrong and, at best, you are going to have a losing run. At worst, you can end up in hospital.

Feeding regularly, then, is important and the timing of it vital for success. Make a mistake, and you are going nowhere. But this constant intake has its issues – not the least being how to get it down if you really don't fancy it.

Cyclists are fussy. It's what they do well. All of them.

Food is one element you have to have ticked close to the top of the To Do list. But liking what is going into your tum certainly helps the process. Despite what the ads tell you, some of these 'highly nutritious and delicious' gels and bars are, um, yucky. Some riders simply do not like them, which becomes a bit of an issue on a long day in the saddle. Everyone has different needs and likes, and some truly great cyclists have food habits that would involve social services if you fed your kids on such a programme. Let's talk jelly! (Or, if you really insist, Jello!)

Dan Lloyd, who sometimes commentates with me, told me how, as a newbie racing for the Cervélo test team, he committed what was a cardinal sin. He nicked his leader's lunch! Kind of.

Cruising into a feed station is a precarious business, as we know. Pace, timing, bike-handling skills and determination all count if you're going to make a tidy collect without stopping. The juggling begins as you shoulder your prize and begin rummaging for nosh.

Dan executed what he regarded as the perfect take and soon found enough road space to sit up and cruise with his hands off the bars and the bag on his belly. He began foraging. 'You have got to be kidding me,' said his expression. 'F--king jelly sweets!!! Is this a f--king joke?' said his mouth. Dan took the full water bottles and a small tin of Coke. His arms did the talking next as he flung the huge candy-bag towards the enthusiastic roadside fans.

He began to drift back to the team car to get something useful to eat. Just as he knocked off the speed, with feeding riders passing him and stuffing provisions in mouth and pocket, David Millar cruised by, swearing. Seeing Dan bagless, David assumed he'd missed a collect and slammed a full bag into his chest. 'Here's some shit.' Then he went on the radio. The smile on Dan's face after being serviced by his team leader soon disappeared as his earpiece crackled to life. It was the Directeur Sportif: 'Guys, whoever has collected Dave's Haribo, can you please hand it over. *Now!*' Dan said nothing and rode on with the slightly strange expression of forced innocence one adopts going through Customs at airports: 'I have absolutely nothing to declare', said his face.

If you are surprised by Haribo and cans of Coke, then add to the list women's tights. On a hot day a can of chilled soft drink is one thing, but a pair of tights filled with crushed ice is a whole different level of satisfaction. It's a true example of secondary design. Filled with crushed ice, a pair of tights sits nicely on the back of the neck and as the water runs down it cools both jugulars, anterior and exterior. If tights – or 'ladies' panty-hose,' as Sean always calls them – didn't exist, you'd have to invent them, just to cool down a cyclist on a hot day.

THIRSTY?

Heat and dehydration are a couple of the biggest problems a rider has to overcome on a Tour de France stage in the middle of July. Great care has to be taken to constantly top up with liquids. You often see a whole team, all eight riders, take a sip from their bidon at the same time because their Directeur Sportif has just reminded them over the team radio to take a drink. Hydration is so critical to the correct functioning of the body that it has been the centre of much research. One of the findings is that the signals your body gives you – thirst – arrive too late. This means that if you are experiencing thirst, you are in fact already too late to maintain full function. A top athlete is already behind the ideal hydration curve. For this reason, teams are constantly nagging riders to drink on a schedule tailored to the day and their need or exertion levels. It's all very scientific. It wasn't always the case.

The effects of thirst can make a rider do silly things. Over the years there have been many teams sponsored by beer companies, Pelforth (a fine drop) being one of the better known in the early 1960s. One of these teams had the bright, yet rather sneaky, idea of hobbling the opposition by putting out a trestle table lined up with iced glasses full of beer on the approach to a series of late climbs. The vessels were real glass, not plastic – which these days you're not allowed to take on to the course. And they looked so tempting, all frosted up on a blisteringly hot day. To the thirsty peloton, this was irresistible stuff. Many fell on the frosty vessels, heartily swigging down what must have been pure nectar. Half an hour later, all those who'd succumbed to the temptation had completely had it. The pack was decimated and half the peloton trundled in some minutes behind the leaders. Of course, the riders who were in on the trick stuck to their water rations and came in ahead of their rivals – and were rewarded with a few cold beers beyond the line.

In the old days, they'd hand out almost anything. Unlike today, riders did not enjoy the same levels of support in terms of being fed and watered. Indeed, it was a frequent sight to witness riders stopping to take a dash into a café or bar and just grab the first thing they could find. On a fateful day in 1967, one of Tom Simpson's fellow riders did just that. Time being precious, he laid the bike down and ran into a small tavern, simply grabbing the closest bottle to hand. This turned out to be cognac. Despite this, it was handed around the leading riders, who were simply grateful to dampen tongues that were as dry as stone. Later that day poor Tom died of a cardiac arrest on the slopes of Ventoux. The autopsy found traces of amphetamines in his system and, of course, alcohol. The press thus proceeded to mark the man in two ways as a result. It's true that dehydration on a punishingly hot day coupled with amphetamines proved to be a lethal combination, but Tom Simpson was no alcoholic; he was simply a man at the very limit of his resources, who had nothing else to quench the kind of raging thirst that thankfully few of us will ever be forced to experience.

DINNER TIME

Apart from the delights of calling the world's most dramatic and beautiful sport, the thing that preoccupies commentators most is food. OK . . . and drink. Both types of sustenance vie for position at the top of the priority list – and, to be fair, the first drink of the night is considered a marker for how the rest of the evening is going to progress. Get this bit right, and the remaining downtime off the microphone is likely to be just dandy.

For wine, France is king. Sorry, Italy, you have some spectaculars but *vini francesi* are *i migliori*. But the boot is most definitely on the other foot in the kitchen. Sorry, France, you can keep your Michelin stars and your fancy sauces because when it comes to top nosh, Italy has it. By far.

There was a time when teams wouldn't even bring a chef and catering along to races in Italy. So renowned and predictably excellent is the food in this cradle of culinary civilisation that teams knew they could get fed extremely well either at a roadside café or at a modest hotel. This was all in the days before everyone got a bit weird about nutrition.

Then: An unshaven bloke wearing a string vest calls out through a doorway swinging with wooden beads that mark a vague boundary to his guesthouse kitchen: 'Pasta Arrabiata or risotto? Red or white wine? Help yourself to bread.'

Now: Bloke wearing a shirt with the team logo and a badge marked Doctor before his name: 'Right, here's an antihistamine. Wash it down with this electrolyte pulp. No dinner for you this evening. We have to shift those 600 grams or the numbers won't work on Wednesday…'

As for those of us who push buttons and pens and not pedals, the search for sustenance varies in length according to requirements. In Sean Kelly you find a man extraordinarily content with pizza. In fact, even in France it is his preferred choice. Most nights, annoyingly. Every night, if he could get away with it. I'm sure he went looking for pizza when he raced in South Africa.

Me: 'What is it with pizza all the bleedin' time?'

Sean: 'It covers most food groups all in one go. You have your vegetables, carbohydrates, protein, and even fruit if you go for Hawaiian. Job done.'

There are nights we eat apart.

I follow the advice of a football commentator friend, Jurriaan van Wessem, the son of the head of the Netherlands National Academy of Arts and a man who went AWOL after being sent to study History of Art in Italy. He never returned. Juri says that one should always head for the railway station. Unlike the UK, where an absolute arse called Dr Beeching ripped up the system, Italy kept all its lines, both national and local. So just about everywhere has a station. As trains came before cars, there was usually a hotel of some note nearby to accommodate late arrivals before their journey continued the following day. These places still exist, albeit rather crumbling. Walk in past the exterior flaking paint and signage with letters missing, and you will find a crisply clean place of faded grandeur, at peace with itself. They also usually offer a no-choice menu of spectacular value. As cheap as the chips they don't sell. I walked into one such place on the Tirreno Adriatico, in Civitanova. There was just one man running the place. It was a Sunday night and it was packed. He showed me to a table and without a word put a half-litre carafe of red in front of me along with a dish of spicy olives for me to pick at. What followed were four courses of the most welcome food you can imagine. A hearty chickpea broth. Spaghetti Vongole: white clams, butter, black pepper and some herbs – magical. A fine slice of grilled pork with diced garlic potatoes. Sorbet and a Limoncello. The bill was €15. I nearly wept.

Sometimes I do have pizza with Sean. They are, of course, excellent in Italy.

'SHAKEN, BUT HOW STIRRED HE IS, IS ANYBODY'S GUESS.'

14
HAVING FUN – THE SECRET TO CYCLING COMMENTARY

I learned a lot from David Duffield – undoubtedly, one of the finest cycling commentators.

Duffers, as he was known to his friends, came into cycling via the bike trade. Here was the man, unsung, who helped to bring the Raleigh Chopper into our world. He had to fight for it too. The bosses were into 'proper bikes', but David was convinced the 'American cruiser' had a place in Europe. It was a huge success. Then came BMX. David couldn't believe how much fun these were, and again he had to fight to get what looked like 'little bikes for big kids' off the ground. On both counts he was a genius who took a modest salary yet made millions for the companies he worked for, including Raleigh, Halfords, Falcon, Claud Butler, Pashley and Muddyfox among others. When Alex Moulton, who'd developed the ingenious suspension system that enabled the Austin Mini to succeed, decided to have a go at bicycles, it was David Duffield who got the call to help develop the market for his revolutionary small-wheel commuter. Everybody knew the man and knew he was the touchstone for anything cutting edge in the business.

Such out-of-the-box thinking might be part of the reason he became the established 'alternative' voice of cycling. The hugely popular Phil Liggett was at ITV and had wrapped up the Tour de France gig and more for the millennia. Four-time Individual Pursuit World Champion Hugh Porter was at the BBC, meaning the Olympics, Commonwealth Games and most other major events were spoken for too. That left David Duffield with the remnants. 'The crumbs on the plate – but tasty crumbs', as he put it. He was, as he said himself, *The Third Man*; he used to sing out the tune from the classic film for comedic effect on entering the office – followed, for some reason, by 'Morning, campers!'

Duffers was from Wolverhampton, the heartland of manufacturing. The other two Midland Mafia boys had wrapped up the cycling gigs on television, so David was left with the rest of the duties on offer. This usually involved tribune work; calling races home for the benefit of the crowd in market squares or city parks. He was *the* live voice on-site. So while Liggett and Porter were embedded inside their cosy studios with lip mikes and headphones, David was under a brolly on the public address system, geeing up a crowd of damp fans at, say, the Lincoln Grand Prix. If you attended a UK cycling event from the 1970s onwards, then you knew David's voice.

This was a man who stood tall in so many ways – almost 2m (6ft 6in) in his stockinged feet, with a fingertip-to-fingertip span bigger than his height. He would extend his canoe-paddle hands on thin wrists in every direction and the returned handshakes were warm and frequent. You couldn't go to a bike show and walk three paces with him before someone would shout: 'Duffers!!!' And another long chat would ensue with either a fan or one of the many thousands of folk he was connected to in the business. He was a genuine gent with a big heart and a bigger sense of mischief. I loved him.

So how did he move into the cosy studio of Eurosport? Well, back in 1989 when the channel started, it was, frankly, regarded as a little lowbrow by the other two busy boys on terrestrial TV. They passed David's name to a desperate producer in Paris who needed someone to call home the Milan–San Remo on the new channel. David jumped at the chance and never let go of the position. He grew with Eurosport and became the most prolific commentator of his generation. Sure, he was 'only' on satellite TV, but he didn't care because the races were plentiful. He was a boy in a toyshop and the door was now locked behind him on this gig.

Without the strictures of ITV or the BBC, Duffers developed his own style. In the absence of any production guidance, or even a co-commentator, and with hours and hours of long stage races to fill, he relied on his experience on the PA in Preston and beyond – and that stood him in good stead. Being able to regale the audience with his musings and his tales both big and small from the cycling world, he was a wonder to behold. That, coupled with a rapacious appetite for good food and, ahem, the products of the grape and hop, meant that he could fill dead air like no other. And he took this all very seriously.

In the early days of our pairings, he said to me with a wink and a tap on the side of the nose: 'Tomorrow we are in the Algarve, so tonight we are going to sample a bit of it!' We were to voice the race from a studio just outside London, but that night David and I went to a Portuguese restaurant called O Galo Negro. It was in Lewisham, I believe. Anyway, we had Portuguese wine and spiced chicken, all written down in his notebook with the correct pronunciations. He then informed the owner that he would be mentioning his place on television the following day and would he like to seal the deal with one of his finest port wines? This was a given. David enquired after the owner's original place of birth and other bits and bobs. The next day, before we went on air, David said: 'We won't be saying we are actually in Portugal, but we won't be saying we are not there either. We will, however, be helping the audience to *believe* we are there. Leave it to me.'

I did my welcome and teed the race up. David then had his moment: 'Thanks, Carlton. Well, I'd just like to take a moment to thank our friend Jose Balan from Tavira, whose Frango Temporado is the talk of the town; it's spicy chicken and was all washed down with a spectacular Galitos Red – lots of blackcurrants and liquorice notes. . .' And on he went. There was nothing happening in the race because the breakaway had gone early, we had three hours to kill and David's trip had not only covered 20 minutes of quiet time but had also framed the day and made the audience assume we were in Portugal, adding credibility to the rest of the week's broadcast. Genius.

Sadly, David is no longer with us. I presented a eulogy at a celebration of his life in the spring of 2016. The mood was naturally sombre as I began with: 'David told me a few secret truths about cycling. Many of which I can't pass on. But one thing I can share is this: He once told me that Lucozade Sport, in a see-through bottle, is exactly the same colour as Scotch and Ginger!' The place erupted.

Having fun is what life is all about. And David knew that. He showed me that being on the telly as a commentator is not about fitting in, it's about being yourself. Anyone can impersonate a commentator, but being a unique one is the goal. 'Be yourself,' he told me, 'and if they like you, then you will fly. Never forget that nobody else will ever be as good at being you as you are.' So I duly made a pact with David, who I'm sure still hangs around, to simply be myself. So far, it has stood me in good stead.

15
RELATIONS MOST PUBLIC

My dad, Bill, was a mortar bomber in the Korean War. His role was to protect infantry on the front line just 200m (656ft) up ahead. This made Billy-lad, as he's known, a prime target. Dad doesn't like to talk about it too much, but he has said that the order 'Fix bayonets!!!', as they were about to be overrun, still wakes him up at night.

'In any battle, things can get a bit messy. What matters is how you cope...'

Things indeed got a bit messy for Team Sky not that long ago. They coped . . . rather well.

The bloodhounds of journalism have the word *investigative* as part of their job title. This is a role that can be useful to society, changing lives for the good. It is also an excuse for being a royal arse. The trouble with journalists – and as a commentator I am one myself – is that they need a story. They don't do this just for fun. They need to meet deadlines and they need to feed their kids . . . or pet crocodiles. Controversy is pure currency to the investigative journalist, and so a sniff of blood is likely to get these guys attacking in packs.

As a result, it's hard to get *anything* out of well-drilled teams like Sky or Team Ineos, as they are now. Their view of all journalists seems to be that you can't offer a nibble to a hungry beast without the possibility of losing an arm. So the shop is closed.

But if Sky operates in lockdown, it's because they would rather let their racing do the talking. And sometimes the racing does an awful lot of talking indeed. I'm not just referring to winning Grand Tours. No. Watch them. Always. They are *soooo* clever.

Give them an inch and they will take 49.71 miles – or 80km. They proved this during the 101st Giro d'Italia in 2018. Froome's masterful domination when he launched his solo attack with this distance remaining on Stage 19 up to Bardonecchia was something to behold. The Sky machine working beautifully to put the hurt on the entire field and tee up Froome's spectacular launch. This was strategy planned and delivered – but earlier in the season, away from the eyes of many fans and at a much lesser event, Sky's relentless planning and workings were, for me, no less impressive.

In December 2017 the journalists at the French newspaper *Le Monde* scented blood and for the following six months Sky were on high alert, aware that the pack was ready to pounce.

According to tests carried out at La Vuelta in 2017, race winner Chris Froome had elevated levels of the permitted but restricted anti-asthma drug Salbutamol in his system. The case caused uproar, not least because Froome was adamant that he had done nothing wrong and would race on during an appeals process.

Sky backed their man, but as the furore grew with each passing month on the way to the Grand Tour season, the pressure to withdraw from racing must have been close to unbearable.

The noise of protest and disdain grew louder after Froome won the Giro d'Italia, becoming the simultaneous holder of all three Grand Tours. On the approach to the Tour de France, former winner Bernard Hinault called for riders to strike if Froome were to take the start. The furore forced the race organisers, the Amaury Sport Organisation (ASO), to issue a statement saying Froome would not be allowed to register to race. The following day, just five days before the start of the Tour de France, both the World Anti-Doping Agency (WADA) and cycling's world governing body the UCI announced that Froome had no case to answer. The test readings were deemed explainable and valid so the four-time Tour de France winner would race after all. Froome did not win the 105th edition of the Tour de France, but he helped teammate Geraint Thomas to the prize and secured a podium for himself. On the face of it, this was an amazing result for a rider competing against the fatigue of the three Grand Tour wins and the sheer pressure of the public antagonism whipped up by the Salbutamol enquiry. Of course he was attempting to win a fourth Grand Tour in a row, but his still very impressive third place and the win for his friend Geraint Thomas must have felt like a very special achievement all the same.

It had been a long process to establish Froome's innocence. Many of us in the media got bruised along the way for refusing to condemn him before the appeal had been completed. The PR and strategy departments for Team Sky must have emerged from the bunker on that sunny Monday with battle scars aplenty but medals on their chests. This had been a long campaign and they achieved some remarkable things – but I had witnessed their effectiveness a little earlier, on a cold mid-February day in Andalucia in 2018.

The Tour of Andalucia may not be at the top of the list of great events even for dedicated cycling fans. But for Sky, the race was a vital element in the process of bringing Chris Froome back into competitive racing after two months of press speculation and vitriol, and at the same time reintroducing the public to a man who, let's remind ourselves, was racing under appeal. How would the crowd react? With cups of urine thrown in the rider's direction – as was the case at the Tour de France in the past? Well, just to make sure any piss-toleroes were dealt with effectively, Sky arrived with the only bodyguard in the race. He was at Froome's side whenever he was off the bike.

Despite this, the fans in this racing-mad region of Europe were accepting and intrigued rather than hostile. There was conversation not condemnation in the cafés.

We commentators were fascinated to see how this would pan out. The primary question in our minds was: Would Team Sky allow Froome to win? Surely he needed to build bridges while racing back to Grand Tour form, so to come out winning would likely make life even harder ahead of the Giro. He would be active, we reckoned, but off the radar. We were absolutely right.

Early season races are notoriously difficult affairs to gauge form. Nobody wants to hit their best too early. As a result, you often get great riders at races such as Andalucia who wish to simply find out where they are on their own performance curve. Winning is not necessarily a priority. Froome had been training at altitude in South Africa and so nobody knew quite what to expect. The start list was 'very provisional' right up to its declaration the night before. Nairo Quintana pulled out on the eve of the race.

So Sky had a conundrum: Froome had to test himself in competition – but not win. Too much aggro would follow such a victory. With the Giro looming and the Salbutamol case rolling on, the pressure might just build enough to deny him a start in Italy. Careful planning was needed.

Stage 1 predictably went to the sprinters, Sacha Modolo taking the run into Granada. Then Stage 2 came along, and the first full-on European climbing day of the season, up to Alto de las Allenadas. A group of exceptional quality was battling for the win and ultimately the race lead. Mikel Landa

(Movistar) and Jakob Fuglsang (Astana) were busy, as was Tim Wellens (Lotto-Soudal) and Wout Poels (Sky). Louis León Sánchez (Astana) and Marc Soler (Movistar) were there too, along with Chris Froome.

Froome had put on a familiar burst of pace to bridge to the group that mattered with 1,400m (4,590ft) to go. He was at the rear and Poels up front. There was no need for a radio signal to know when to go for it. Poels launched in the last 500m (1,640ft) and did a double job. Not only did he win a stage to take control of the race, he also deflected attention from Chris Froome, who must have been delighted by his own form.

So Froome was now a contender. Remember, the plan was to race on hard but avoid victory. A difficult balance indeed. There was, I guess you might say, always the chance of an accidental performance just being too good for the plan. And that nearly happened.

Another sprinters' day on Stage 3 gave way to the race's pivotal stage ahead of the finale of the time trial. Froome was looking *very* good. Ooops!

An uphill cobbled finish beckoned to the line at Alcalá de los Gazules. Froome was in contention, and on any 'normal' day he would have been a red-hot favourite. Other riders around him were tiring, so this looked to many like his chance of glory. I took a (perhaps more cynical) view. The individual time trial was beckoning the following day, and I judged that Froome would want to test his time trial legs properly on the last day without also winning the race, which meant he had to shed time on this day. How was he going to do it? I speculated on air that the answer might just lie in a 'puncture of convenience'. And guess what? Within 10 minutes, the cameras cut to Froome standing by his bike in no hurry whatsoever. He managed to lose two minutes.

I imagined the PR department lighting cigars: no pressure on the final day. Poels with a chance to win the race and Froome with a nice time trial against quality opposition, able to go for it without a chance of victory. Job done. Well, almost. Tim Wellens won the race eight seconds clear of Poels, but Sky were as content as they could be. Their main man had passed many tests at this race. He'd faced the public, the media, some sterling opposition and bolstered his own physical and mental condition. Battles well won, though the war continued to rage on many fronts.

'IT'S HEARTBREAK HOTEL OUT THERE AND EVERYONE'S A RESIDENT I'M AFRAID.'

At that initial launch of Team Sky back in 2010, there was a big press conference to reveal the team kit. The black Adidas jersey was a departure from the garish colours favoured by most teams of the time. Much was made of the blue stripe that ran down the back of the jersey from the nape of the neck to the waist. This, declared Dave Brailsford, represented the clear blue water that separated old cycling culture with its dirty, murky history and the new culture that Team Sky championed. Team Sky was at the very forefront, spearheading a squeaky-clean organisation that would not accept anyone to work or ride for them who had been tainted by dubious activities in the past. The blue stripe down the back of the jersey was the line that separated this new team from others, and a line that should never be crossed. Team Sky painted itself as one of the good guys. It also painted itself into a corner, a corner where spotlights glared. This, everyone thought, had better be good . . .

The debate goes on as to whether Sky did, in fact, ever cross the line. What we do know is that at least ethically it seems they were pushing up against it as hard as possible.

16
THE DARK SIDE OF CYCLING

Ever since the sport of racing bicycles began, it's had a murky side. Riders have always sought an advantage over their competitors. For the best, this simply means doing what comes naturally. For those missing a certain competitive percentage or two, the temptation to find an angle in the great chase can mean a step towards the dark side.

'Doping' is a generic term, and it can take many forms. There is a spectrum here. It's not just about needles, pills and potions. No. The word now extends well beyond the chemical, and includes Accommodation Doping and Mechanical Doping.

So, cycling: let's be straight about how bent it was. And is.

For those of us who love the sport and defend it, modern doping offences leave us wincing. It is the most rigorously tested sport on the planet. Which means cheats have a significant chance of being caught. When they are, it is wounding for us fans. That said, some of the older ruses can indeed raise a smile. Let's call it Pirate Syndrome; think Blackbeard rather than Pantani (aka Il Pirata) for a moment.

Kids love a tale of derring-do with a bit of swashbuckling, whatever that means. Truth is, pirates were evil murderous marauders responsible for some truly heinous crimes. Time has softened their reputation to the near comedic. So it is with some early cycling cheats.

CHOO-CHOO CHEATS

1903 saw the first Tour de France, with Maurice Garin the inaugural winner. It was a small band of brothers who survived that first amazing test of endurance. Garin beat Lucien Pothier by a margin just shy of three hours, with Fernand Augereau a further hour and a half behind in third.

Garin and Pothier had a fine year getting paid for talking about the great event in smoky cafés and packed town halls. They ate and drank well, being fêted throughout the land. Unfortunately, this celebrity regime took a toll and then, in the blink of an eye, it was suddenly time to defend the title. . . Ah!

Maurice and Lucien had both fallen victim to the 'Winning and Dining' lifestyle. They were a bit fat. Neither was in the mood, or shape, to go through the hell of Le Tour again so soon. Thus it is rumoured that Maurice, Lucien and others decided to seek help – in the form of steam and railway timetables.

The Tour was dogged with controversy and nine competitors were disqualified for, among other things, being pulled by or even sitting inside cars.

The original results saw the miraculous Maurice Garin successfully defend his title, with Pothier again coming second – though by a much narrower margin of 6 minutes 28 seconds. Hippolyte Aucouturier won four of the six enormous stages that circled France to finish fourth behind the winner's brother, César Garin, who made up the podium. Cosy.

The results weren't to last, however, because the French cycling union, L'Union Vélocipédique de France, decided to interview competitors and witnesses, and then, in December 1904, disqualified the first four finishers.

The UVF never revealed its reasoning, but there are rumours of Garin taking a train. This claim was confirmed many years later by a man who, as a boy, had heard Garin tell this story.

A total of 12 riders were disqualified. Henri Cornet, who originally finished fifth, was now blowing his own trumpet as the newly declared winner.

Things had to change and for the 1905 Tour rules were tightened, and the scrutiny of results, and just about everything else, now became the norm. Sadly, despite this welcome rigour, cycling now had an image problem regarding integrity. It still has.

BAAAA-D BOYS!

In more modern times, it's said racers in Ireland used to be able to hire a flock of sheep to 'help out'. Apparently in the 1970s the going rate was equivalent to about €35. Timing was of the essence to pull this one off. The chosen rider made his breakaway ahead of the appointed location, whereupon a gate was opened and a flock of sheep went about its business moving from one field to another via the country road that formed part of the course. Sean Kelly told me once, with a twinkle in his eye, 'That could gain a man as much as ten minutes. That's a good night out in Carrick!' I still don't know if he's pulling my leg on this one.

'HE'S GOT WELDER'S GOGGLES ON AT THE MOMENT AND HE'S WHITE HOT.'

STICKY STICK DOPING

It's in time trialling that most of the questions have been raised about riders gaining an unfair advantage. It's the race of truth – just one man against the clock – which gives it a certain purity. But if one rider has an outstanding ride, questions are sure to be asked. One such incident came in the Milk Race in the 1960s when one rider recorded an extraordinary time that had jaws dropping all the way down to the tarmac. Nobody could work out how he'd done it. No rules appeared to have been broken.

The secret came down to a simple broom handle. The rules in a time trial dictate that a team car can draw alongside a rider but it must remain 2m (6ft 6in) from him. Encouragement is all that is allowed. The 2-metre distance is a hard one to bridge. But with a little good housekeeping it can be managed by the unscrupulous. It turned out that the broom kept in the car was not for tidying up. It had another use. At any opportune moment the broom handle was extended out of the car's rear window and the end hooked behind the back of the rider's seat post. Tidy!

ACCOMMODATION DOPING

Are you all sleeping comfortably? Then I'll begin. In 2015 the term 'Accommodation Doping' was first used after Team Sky's 'marginal gains' drive extended to the sleeping arrangements for Richie Porte, the Giro d'Italia team leader. Rather than being billeted in hotels with his teammates, Porte had a luxury motorhome parked outside each of the overnight stops. It meant the same room and conditions for Porte throughout the race. Same bed, quilt and pillow, teddy bear, night light . . . you name it. All this without the need to pack, unpack or check in anywhere. Luxury.

Other teams objected. Small teams could not afford to copy the Sky model, and were not happy at all, complaining about the potential advantage. This gathered some critical momentum in the press.

RIGHT: *It's a great job … and no, you can't have it!* A sports broadcaster since the mid-1980s, my first live on-site cycling commentary was the 1998 VTT Tour de France … that's Velo Tout Terrain, or mountain biking to you and me. I was finally let loose on a Grand Tour in 2005 and have covered more than 300 cycling events.

BELOW: *No entry fee, you just have to climb a mountain.* This photo was taken from the roof of the commentary position on Monte Zoncolan, the finish of stage 14 on the Giro 2018. The mountainside probably had 300,000 people dotted all over it who bore rain, sleet and chilly temperatures. Maximum gradient: 22%. Spectators' enthusiasm: 100%.

BELOW: *The Grand Tour caravan in all its glory.* There are around 4,500 people involved in bringing the Tour de France to life on every day of the race. Most of them seem to be in this shot. You can see the course finish in the top left, and all the team coaches and support vehicles that have just driven the course with bikes on the roof.

ABOVE: *Erm … did I go a bit far there Sean? Sean!?* Sean Kelly is a legend. A Grand Tour winner who claimed nine monuments as well as the Paris–Nice seven times in a row! No wonder they call him The King. On any Tour day we might be together for 15 hours travelling, broadcasting and dining. No surprise that sometimes, just sometimes, I get on his nerves. The man's a saint.

BELOW: *Yep … we're lost.* Kelly is old-school, in the best possible sense. He trusts instinct and he's usually right. It's been like that his whole career: he can read a race like no other, and he's still doing it as a commentator. He leaves the flannel to me… and occasionally mops up the mess. It works well.

ABOVE LEFT: *The camera-bike genius of Patrice Diallo.* The ground camera operators have a difficult task: the route is strictly defined and there is real a tension in finding the shots without interfering with the race. While Patrice Diallo doesn't operate the camera he makes sure the cameramen he pilots get the very best out of every moment. Merci maestro.

ABOVE RIGHT: *This is not a bike rack …* Pascal Lino mildly troubled by 'fans' in 1997. These days a digital delay is built into TV transmissions, so far fewer bums make it to air; the director has about seven seconds to play with so he can select a less 'cheeky' shot. It also means riders' blushes are saved during 'comfort breaks'. Fan exuberance makes for an amazing atmosphere, provided everyone behaves. © *Getty Images*

BELOW: *Devilish hijinks.* Didi Senft has been dressing as the mountain devil on Grand Tours since 1993. He disappeared from our screens a few years back after he signed a sponsorship deal and was cut from TV broadcasts by race organisers, but he's been back on air after removing the unofficial logos. He must hold some kind of selfie record as he is mobbed by fans wherever he goes. © *Getty Images*

Kirby CODEC

Stage 1 — profile: `1 / • 4 •`
/201 FONTENAY
103 103 45 [103] (215) QST 29
45 184 215

No.	Rider	Team
103	GAVIRIA	QST
111	SAGAN	BOH
144	KITTEL	TKA
95	KRISTOFF	UAD
201	LAPORTE	COF
163	GROENEWEGEN	TLJ
31	MATTHEWS	SUN
194	DEGENKOLB	TFS
121	FUGLSANG	AST
114	MAJKA	BOH

Froome crash Quintana tech
Yates held up

Stage 2 — profile: `2 / 4 • •`
/185 MOUILLERON
111 111 217 [103] (183) QST 34
183 195 217

No.	Rider	Team
111	SAGAN	BOH
52	COLBRELLI	TBM
51	DEMARE	GFC
171	GREIPEL	LTS
95	KRISTOFF	UAD
213	DUPONT	WGG
78	VALVERDE	MOV
216	PASQUALON	WGG
194	DEGENKOLB	TFS
104	GILBERT	QST

Late crashes!
out: 127 196

Stage 3 — profile: `3 / I I`
/35.5 CHOLET
87 111 217 [36] ⊘ BMC 30c 87
TTT

Team	Time		Team	Time	No.
BMC	38.46		ALM	1'15	103
SKY	4"		TLJ	1'15	111
QST	7"		TFS	1'16	171
MTS	9"		UAD	1'38	163
SUN	11"		GFC	1'42	144
EFD	35"		FST	1'46	216
BOH	50"		TDE	1'51	95
AST	51"		LTS	1'52	194
TKA	52"		DDD	1'52	217
MOV	53"		WGG	2'24	213
TBM	1'06		COF	3'25	

1st OLY Ch in Yellow
Big losers!

Stage 4 — /19 ... 18

Stage 8 — profile: `8 / 4 4`
/181 AMIENS
87 111 197 [36] (186) QST 28

Gaviria + Greipel relegated
Tony Martin out. Dan Martin crash

Stage 9 — profile: `9 / •`
/156 ROUBAIX
87 111 197 [36] (185) QST 26
168 174

x 15 sectors 21.7km
Porte out cd carbone

Stage 10 — profile: `10 / 40 HC`
/158 GRAND BORNAND
87 111 101 [26] (87) MOV 78c
x 21

No.	Rider	Team	
101	ALAPHILIPPE	QST	8
55	IZAGUIRRE.J	TBM	32
188	TAARAMAE	TDE	1
87	Van AVERMAET	BMC	83
134	PAUWELS	DDD	68
181	CALMEJANE	TDE	91
91	MARTIN.D	UAD	204
166	ROGLIC	TLJ	21
152	GAUDU	GFC	51
8	THOMAS	SKY	71

Colombiere
Uran (i) GVA !!!

Stage 11 — /1C x3 8

Stage 15 — profile: `15 / 3 2 •`
/181 CARCASSONNE
8 111 101 [26] (114) MOV 29
x 29

No.	Rider	Team
126	CORT NIELSEN	AST
55	IZAGUIRRE.J	TBM
191	MOLLEMA	TFS
128	VALGREN	AST
197	SKUJINS	TFS
58	POZZOVIVO	TBM
181	CALMEJANE	TDE
114	MAJKA	BOH
33	ARNDT	SUN
192	BERNARD	TFS

Sagan's 100k Green
Moscon out of race.
Hitting rider

Stage 16 — profile: `16 / 4 4 3`
/218 BAG de LUCHON
8 111 101 [26] (104) TBM
x 41 ... after 1 hour!

No.	Rider	Team
101	ALAPHILIPPE	QST
54	IZAGUIRRE.G	TBM
61	YATES.A	MTS
191	MOLLEMA	TFS
58	POZZOVIVO	TBM
162	GESSINK	TLJ
128	VALGREN	AST
115	MUHLBERGER	BOH
77	SOLER	MOV
26	LATOUR	ALM

Tearpass Farmers delay
Gilbert crash: Out bke
Yates crash: OK

Stage 17 — profile: `17 / HC`
/65 ST.LARY SOULAN
8 111 101 [26] (125) MOV
x 32 ... broke apart

No.	Rider	Team	
71	QUINTANA	MOV	151
91	MARTIN.D	UAD	201
8	THOMAS.G	SKY	95
166	ROGLIC	TLJ	132
32	DUMOULIN.T	SUN	52
161	KRUIJSWIJK	TLJ	107
2	BERNAL	SKY	194
1	FROOME	SKY	111
75	LANDA	MOV	15
41	ZAKARIN	TKA	213

Col de Portet
G looks like a champ

Stage 18 — /1... 8 63

This is the Kirby CODEC. My notes on every stage of a tour in a single page. Each 'cell' details the stage number and type: red for climbs, green for sprints and orange for time-trials. Then the course profile, which shows the categories of the climbs, dots for sprints as well as the distance of the day in kilometres and the destination. Added to this are the jerseys, combativity award winners, leading team and temperature. The breakaway is noted as well as the top 10 with a dotted line marking the top 5.

Stage 5 — 204 QUIMPER

87	111	197	36	197	QST 26c

218 43 138 173 181 183 197 203

QST	111	SAGAN	BOH
BOH	52	COLBRELLI	TBM
LTS	104	GILBERT	QST
EGCMTLJ	78	VALVERDE	MOV
TKA	101	ALAPHILIPPE	QST
ON WGG	91	MARTIN.D	UAD
UAD	87	Van AVERMAET	BMC
OLB TFS	36	KRAGH And'n	SUN
WGG	216	PASQUALON	WGG
WGG	51	NIBALI	TBM

Matthews fever DNS
'G' 12km Froome 14th

Stage 6 — 181 Mur De Bretagne

87	111	197	36	185	QST 26c

47 185 186 208 217

91	MARTIN.D	UAD
26	LATOUR	ALM
78	VALVERDE	MOV
101	ALAPHILIPPE	QST
114	MAJKA	BOH
61	YATES.A	MTS
191	MOLLEMA	TFS
111	SAGAN	BOH
8	THOMAS	SKY
166	ROGLIC	TLJ

Wind = splits
Dumoulin 20" pen. auto paced

Stage 7 — 231 CHARTRES

87	111	197	36	47	QST 29c

215 ..... ☹ 47

163	GROENEWEGEN	TLJ
103	GAVIRIA	QST
111	SAGAN	BOH
151	DEMARE	GFC
201	LAPORTE	COF
194	DEGENKOLB	TFS
67	IMPEY	MTS
171	GREIPEL	LTS
216	PASQUALON	WGG
131	CAVENDISH	DDD

Kittel said no!
Huge power win 163

Stage 12 — 175 ALPE D'HUEZ

8	111	101	26	161	MOV 28

x30 ...161 solo

SKY	8	THOMAS	SKY
N.T SUN	32	DUMOULIN	SUN
SKY	21	BARDET	ALM
BMC	1	FROOME	SKY
MTS	75	LANDA	MOV
UAD	166	ROGLIC	TLJ
COF	51	NIBALI	TBM
ALM	121	FUGLSANG	AST
TBM	71	QUINTANA	MOV
MOV	161	KRUIJSWIJK	TLJ

Madeleine, Croix de Fer
G-whiz! Nibali out.

Stage 13 — 169 VALENCE

8	111	101	26	86	MOV 30

17 86 174 202

111	SAGAN	BOH
95	KRISTOFF	UAD
151	DEMARE	GFC
194	DEGENKOLB	TFS
87	Van AVERMAET	BMC
106	LAMPAERT	QST
126	CORT NIELSEN	AST
216	PASQUALON	WGG
52	COLBRELLI	TBM
15	PHINNEY	EFD

Sagan again!
Many sprinters gone

Stage 14 — 188 MENDE

8	111	101	26	198	MOV 26

x31

122	FRAILE	AST
101	ALAPHILIPPE	QST
198	STUYVEN	TFS
111	SAGAN	BOH
83	CARUSO	BMC
34	GESCHKE	SUN
203	EDET	COF
181	CALMEJANE	TOE
67	IMPEY	MTS
174	DE GENDT	LTS

Dan Martin :)
Adam Yates :(

Stage 19 — 200 LARUNS

8	111	101	26	75	TBM 30

21 41 54 68 72 75
101 103 114 123 141

GFC	166	ROGLIC	TLJ
COF	8	THOMAS	SKY
UAD	21	BARDET	ALM
DDD	91	MARTIN.D	UAD
TBM	114	MAJKA	BOH
QST	32	DUMOULIN	SUN
OLB TFS	75	LANDA	MOV
BOH	1	FROOME	SKY
EFD	161	KRUIJSWIJK	TLJ
WGG	141	ZAKARIN	TKA

Last!
ASPIN.TOURMALET.AUBISQUE
Roglic up to 3rd.
Froome off podium

Stage 20 — 31 ESPELETTE

8	111	101	26		MOV 14

iTT

32	DUMOULIN	SUN
1	FROOME	SKY
8	THOMAS	SKY
4	KWIATKOWSKI	SKY
36	KRAGH And'n	SUN
105	JUNGELS	QST
141	ZAKARIN	TKA
166	ROGLIC	TLJ
77	SOLER	MOV
65	HEPBURN	MTS

Decider !?
Prince of Wales
King of France

Stage 21 — 116 CHAMPS-ELYSEES

8	111	101	26	91	28

15 22 86 147 185 218

95	KRISTOFF	UAD
194	DEGENKOLB	TFS
151	DEMARE	GFC
132	BOASSON Hag'	DDD
201	LAPORTE	COF
107	RICHEZE	QST
52	COLBRELLI	TBM
111	SAGAN	BOH
216	PASQUALON	WGG
173	De BUYST	LTS

Mab Mwyaf Cymru
"G"

ABOVE LEFT: *On-the-bike refuelling.* Early riders got very little support on the road. They had to ride carrying spare equipment, often slept in churches and grabbed whatever they could from markets and cafés … sometimes without paying! It's said bars regarded it as an honour. Jules Merviel won stage 7 of the 1930 Tour de France, 222km (138miles) from Bordeaux to Hendaye. He's not celebrating here – the race was still on! © *Offside/L'Equipe*

ABOVE RIGHT: *Rock and roll.* I watched every stage of the 1978 Tour de France from the factory canteen in La Haye du Puits, where I had a summer job driving a forklift. Bernard Hinault took the first of his five Tour de France titles. He looked like a rock star and was as hard as they come. The Sex Pistols released *Never Mind the Bollocks*, and suddenly I had a soundtrack and a sporting hero to carry me through my teens. Magic. © *Getty Images*

BELOW: *The Rule of Three!* 2018 saw Geraint Thomas add his Tour de France title to Chris Froome's Giro, and this was followed by Simon Yates winning La Vuelta. For the first time ever we saw all three Grand Tours won by three different riders from the same nation in a single season. © *Getty Images*

ABOVE: *What a relief!* Working in the commentary booth can be cramped, hot and stuffy so you need to keep hydrated. And that has to go somewhere. When the advert breaks come you have three minutes to pay a call or maybe swap a few thoughts with a colleague. Sometimes you can do both … but only if the plastic pissoir has been stationed close to the commentary position.

BELOW LEFT: *You are what you wear.* I've always been passionate about cycling and one of my first bikes was a Carlton Corsa, obviously, in 'Polychromatic Mauve', which I used to ride wearing a duffel coat as I delivered newspapers around the Derbyshire borders. These days I ride more sophisticated machinery and my favourite brand is Colnago. My attire is different, too…

BELOW RIGHT: *So kind of Sir Brad to bring his mad uncle along to the velodrome* … The first time I worked with Brad I was in full flow at Lee Valley. He smacked me on the backside and said 'Alright Kirbs!' He then plopped the headset on and away he went, natural as you like.

ABOVE: *Writing partners in crime.* For the last two years Robbie Broughton and I have been working on this book. Robbie loved my company so much he moved to Mallorca, but I tracked him down. He lives at the foot of the amazing Sa Batalla climb, and we often ride up to the café at the top where a poster of Sean Kelly stares at us while we eat almond cake.

BELOW: *Nope ... sorry ... definitely not swapping!* Whenever I call a race, one thing remains the same: my deep love for the world of cycling in all its racing forms. At the track, up a mountain or on a city criterium it doesn't matter ... it's just the most wonderful form of sporting endeavour. I feel privileged to be involved.

Under the existing rules, teams were required to take as their location for the night of each stage the hotel booking that had been arranged by the race organisers. The quality of the hotels does vary dramatically. Tales and complaints about a lack of air conditioning and missing mosquito nets on certain stops abound. But any imbalance on a particular night is deemed to even itself out in terms of quality and comfort over the full run of a three-week Grand Tour. Sky had simply figured a way of avoiding all this variation for their leader.

After due consideration, in stepped the UCI and banned the practice.

So there is now a detailed list of accommodation issued at the start of each race, which must be adhered to at all times by all teams and all riders. It's a handy document indeed. Especially as you now know exactly where your enemy is sleeping. And with this list, if you are evil, your rival might find it potentially difficult to sleep. Game on for the naughty.

If you can't speed yourself up, slow your opponent down. You don't need sheep. Just stop your rival counting any himself. A tired rider is a slow rider. There have been numerous complaints by teams of night-time noise being used as a weapon. Hard to prove of course, but it is remarkable how many revellers, partygoers and indeed even live bands have found themselves outside some major team hotels in the small hours of a Tuesday morning, the date of which seems of no apparent significance. Usually in Italy.

Of course, every day of the year has a saint allocated to it. This can provide a lame, if half decent and wily, excuse: 'Ah, sorry. Today we celebrate Saint Cuthbert the Unruly. It's in the diary. Have a look!'

HELICOPTER DOPING

The 1984 Giro d'Italia remains one of the most controversial of all time. There were two main protagonists. Step forward the bespectacled Laurent 'The Professor' Fignon, the Frenchman who had won the Tour de France the previous year. And then in the blue corner was the popular local choice: the Italian Francesco Moser, who had already broken the hour record that year as well as being victorious at Milan–San Remo. The Italians do like their fellow countrymen to win their national race, and everyone was speculating that Fignon was fitter than his Italian counterpart. The French press were livid, accusing the organiser, Vincenzo Torriani, of drawing up a parcours that was fairly flat by Giro standards and cancelling mountain stages in order to favour either Moser or his fellow Italian Beppe Saronni.

When the Stelvio climb, the third highest pass in Europe, reared its head, the officials declared that it was impassable because of snow, despite many commentators of the time claiming that the roads were either clear or could easily be made clear with snow ploughs. Fignon claimed later, 'They knew I was capable of winning the Giro and they made sure I lost. They knew Moser couldn't have followed me.' In his autobiography, Fignon wrote: 'Chains of tifosi had lined the cols to push him up. The referees helped as well by fining me twenty seconds for taking a feed outside the permitted area.'

But more was to come. The final general classification rested on the results of the time trial from Soave to Verona, 42 km (26 miles) of undulating twists and turns, which Moser chose to tackle on his revolutionary time trial machine. He set off ahead of Fignon and was duly followed by a low-flying helicopter, ostensibly there to take TV pictures, though others noted it seemed to be flying so low and so close to Moser that the downdraft blew him along the road. Fignon set off from his start position but was now behind a helicopter. One aircraft was blasting Moser along the road while the other was 'pushing me back', said the Frenchman, who now had to work twice as hard! Moser won convincingly. In fact, his winning margin had everyone shaking their heads in disbelief.

A similar technique has been employed in more recent times in time trials, with team cars riding up as close as they can get behind their rider.

Everyone was asking, 'Why the hell are the team cars getting so close these days?' The answer is that a car driving at 40–50km/h (25–31mph) produces a bow wave aero effect that pushes the air in front of it, helping the rider. There is now a 25m (82ft) rule for following cars.

BANNED KIT

Skinsuits are constantly changing and adapting as the technical development evolves and improves. Some teams spend millions of euros on researching how to improve them, making for a great deal of inequality between teams. One of the biggest advances was the introduction of the phenomenal 'flying squirrel suit'. A piece of aero cloth filled much of the gap between ribcage and underarm and at the same time drew the material down and away from each side of the sternum. In effect, the rider became a wing – a flying squirrel. The aerodynamic effect, according to one coach who tested it in a wind tunnel, was to benefit the rider by an extra 20 watts. The suits were worn by Garmin–Transitions riders during Stage 19 of the 2010 Tour de France. Foul, cried the press. Good point, thought the UCI. The commissaires later deemed the design to be approaching a 'fairing' in contravention of the rules, and the suits were thus banned from future races.

That hasn't stopped the clothing companies from trying to gain other advantages. The shift in focus moved from the shape of the suit to the fabric itself. Movistar appeared to have the edge here. Unfortunately, they just didn't have the riders to match the performance of the cloth. The material would not be the natural choice of an athlete. It looked like something out of *Strictly Come Dancing*. I'm sure the first fitting was a bit of a giggle, but there was sound technical reasoning behind the design. It followed the principle of the dimples on a golf ball: air becomes trapped in the dimples, which makes the surrounding air ride over another cushion of air as opposed to the surface of the body. Interestingly, Movistar used the suit for two seasons before Sky adopted similar technology. When the blue-stripe boys started getting better numbers, the opposition went crazy and sought to have the suits banned. The UCI naturally declared there was no case to answer since the suits had long been in use.

HAIR DOPING ... SERIOUSLY!

All this research and development into aerodynamics in time trialling led a former Formula 1 technician from Red Bull, Professor Tony Purnell, to devote many hours of time and many pounds of money into researching how body hair, and specifically leg hair, can help or hinder a cyclist's aerodynamics. We all know that cyclists shave their legs, but Purnell wanted to find out if this offered any benefit.

A range of experiments conducted at Cambridge University looked into the various options, starting with the difference between completely shaved legs versus hairy legs, then moving on to consider legs that were partially shaved at the front but not at the back, beardy fronts and baldy backs, even beardy sides. Every possible combination was tried and tested in wind tunnels at an exorbitant cost. Was it any use? Well, the conclusion that Purnell reached after many weeks of testing was that, because everyone's hair thickness is different, it's impossible to draw any conclusion at all. However, he did find that with certain types of hair, the ultimate aerodynamic leg shave would involve a bald front of the leg but a hairy back.

The true reason cyclists shave is to make massage less painful and wound dressing easier. And for purely aesthetic reasons, I thank God that no one seems to have taken Professor Purnell's advice.

OTHER TRICKS ... SOME THAT WORK AND SOME THAT DON'T

As well as aerodynamics, cyclists have worked hard for over a century to make their bikes go faster by making adjustments to the frame and wheels.

We all know those riders who struggle to get up a hill or mountain but plummet down at breakneck speeds on the descent because they're just that bit heavier than the others. So, it's not rocket science; we all know that more weight will go against you on the way up, but benefit you on the way down. Hence the use of a lead-filled bidon passed to the rider as he tops the peak of a climb, to be inserted in the bottle cage.

Simple logic also informed the choice of filling tyres with helium rather than just air. It may not make the bike actually float up the mountain, but it could make the whole bike a bit lighter. In this climate of marginal gains, who knows if that extra fraction of a gram of weight saved could make that little difference?

Bladed wheels came on to the market a few years ago. These had a quad spoke of carbon wings that produced a rotor. You could hear them coming from way off. These were expensive and so quite rare. Sadly (since they looked amazing), they were also deemed to be dangerous in the event of a crash. They were duly banned.

Some technology is a little bit more basic. Time trial regulations for some time dictated that the rider's saddle must be absolutely horizontal to avoid the rider gaining an advantage by pushing his backside against an angled seat. On health grounds, this rule has been amended and a pitch variation is now permitted of 10° off the horizontal. Before this allowance, riders struggled to stay planted on their seat and would often be seen taking a moment to shuffle their backside to the rear of the saddle. Tony Martin suffered from 'butt-shuffle' and resorted to rather basic technology to attempt to cure the problem: he glued some sandpaper to the saddle surface. All looked to be going well at first. But what couldn't be seen was the sandpaper tearing through Tony's shorts . . . then the chamois pad . . . and finally his blokey bits. It was a mess. Blood everywhere. I'm pleased to say that few riders have tried this again since. The saddle pitch rule change came as a relief.

THE MAGIC WHEEL

Perhaps a more significant advantage has been taken with some of the mechanical advances that have been hidden. In recent years, there have been some astounding time trials in the Grand Tours, and these have raised eyebrows. When someone like reigning World Time Trial Champion, Tony Martin, is beaten significantly, chins start to wag and questions are asked. In this regard, wheel technology has been the subject of much speculation.

An aero disc on the back wheel can have huge benefits to the aero dynamism of a bike. It is solid and opaque. Could this double-sided disc with a hollow core be used to hide the inner workings of a rogue wheel mechanism?

Organisers insist that all the wheels are the same Mavic model, to avoid any unfair advantage for a team using a more advanced wheel.

There is, however, nothing in the rules that says a regular wheel cannot be employed inside a regulation disc wheel's void. And anyway, what benefit could be gained from the extra weight such a method would employ? Well, let's find out.

There is a particular rear wheel that is rumoured to have been used at the very highest level. This wheel features a spoked wheel inside the regulation Mavic disc. At the heart of it was a magnetic hub with counterweights acting on the spokes, all nicely shrouded by the official solid aero cover.

At speed, the counterweights disengaged from the hub and were flung out to the end of the specially strung spokes to sit at the rim of the wheel. This was said to have a gyroscopic effect, which added to the momentum of the turning wheel, thus giving the rider extra speed. When the rider slowed down – taking a corner, for instance – the weights slid down the spokes and returned to the magnetic hub. Magic.

With the absence of scanners at the time, it is extremely difficult to prove that this technology was ever used, but there has been considerable speculation in France that some of the top teams employed such a wheel, particularly after some of the jaw-droppingly fast time trials seen during major races on occasion.

Such suspicions fired up the French press whenever they thought an outstanding performance needed an explanation beyond the human. It led the French track cycling team's director, Isabelle Gautheron, to accuse British Cycling of using 'magic' as opposed to Mavic wheels. What was it, the question went, that brought Team GB such success at the 2012 Olympics as well as some astounding performances in the Tour de France time trials?

Of course, Sir Dave Brailsford, then performance director of British Cycling, loved the intrigue this speculation generated. The issue was raised at a press conference, where he said to a suddenly hushed press corps: 'I'll tell you what is so special about our wheels. Our wheels . . . are . . . *perfectly*. . . round.' The next day, the French press was alive with questions about how such perfection could be achieved. What methods do les rosbifs have to ensure this impossible perfection they talk of?

Not for the first time, Captain Dave had sunk a speculation fireboat heading his way. He successfully managed to ridicule the French claims – though it's not beyond the realms of possibility that they had some validity, if only in the imagination of the defeated.

ELECTRICAL DRIVE SYSTEMS

Some of the first advances in electric motors within bikes were pioneered by the Italians, who developed a magnetic device hidden within the frame of the bike. Combined with a copper rim to the wheel, this worked as a rudimentary electric motor. Development of this primitive system was eventually abandoned. However, the idea remained alive, and with the power of modern batteries and a direct cam-drive system it is now possible to get an assisted ride while apparently sitting on board a perfectly regular-looking bike. Set up correctly, the motor and battery system is completely contained within the set tube. It can be started and stopped at the touch of a button, allowing the rider a boost when needed for an attack or to simply give them a rest.

This is great news for, say, the club rider who wants to keep up with his fitter mates or a veteran riding with a younger group. So far, so good if all is declared and above board. But what if such a thing were used in the pro peloton? The monster is already with us, I'm afraid.

The discovery of a hidden motor inside the frame of a spare bike used by Femke Van den Driessche at the U23 Cyclo-cross World Championships in January 2016 finally gave some credence to allegations that had been previously dismissed.

Claims of motorised doping in pro cycling go back to 2010, when former pro rider and now head of the Italian Cycling national team Davide Cassani suggested that suspicious hand movements by Fabian Cancellara in that year's Paris–Roubaix and Tour of Flanders indicated that he was engaging a switch to control a motor hidden within the frame of his bike. In a video available on YouTube, he alleges that the Swiss rider was able to power away from his fellow competitors immediately after moving his hand towards his right brake lever. Such claims were never proven.

In the 2014 Vuelta, Ryder Hesjedal, riding for Garmin Sharp at the time, crashed on a descent on Stage 7. As he got up from the road, his bike spun round in a full circle as if it was being powered by its back wheel. It looked to run away from him as Hesjedal struggled to control the bike. It was explained as a high-speed freewheeling rear still moving quickly post-crash. The UCI moved to investigate and found nothing untoward.

RULE BENDING . . . THE GREY AREA

We've pondered the dark side – basically, cheating. Time, then, to consider what are regarded as the 'lesser crimes' in the game of limiting time loss.

The sheer frequency and cheekiness of these mean you may just get away with it.

Cycling as a sport is, of course, magical but occasionally relies on the art of the illusion. This spell can be broken with clumsiness. As with all things in the world of magic, it may take those watching a little time to see how it's done. Once you know the technique, you can figure out the trick. For that is what it is – a plain and simple attempt to confound the audience or referees with sleight of hand. And sometimes, if you do it well and don't take the mickey, even the commissaires, despite knowing the trick, might not mind!

That said, having first referred to the 'magic spanner' in 1996, I'm rather proud that it is now a generic term for a bit of trickery. Let's see how the magic works and consider a few other methods of helping a struggling or unfortunate rider back into the pack.

The team mechanic is hard-working, up early and to bed late, the unsung hero of the team. Washing bikes, fettling them, racking and repairing them. He is the only guy, apart from the rider, who is allowed a physical input during a race; he's the chap with the belly and baggy shorts and fingers as agile as spitting pork sausages on a hot skillet. He's on his knees a lot, frantically trying to replace the rear wheel of the team's star rider who is standing there, hands on skinny hips, with an expression that easily decodes as 'Get a bleedin' move on, Colin, FFS.' After the repair, our Colin can push a rider from a standing start before jumping back in the car. *That push-off is the only physical assist allowable in open competition* – as detailed in UCI Directive 138, Paragraph 6, Subsection 27d – or something like that, you get the idea.

Well, those may well be the rules, but what comes next may well get, ahem, a little bit 'bendy'.

The rider is now up and gone, but the peloton is in the distance. Any energy he can save right now might well be vital to his chances later. This can only mean one thing: the magic is about to begin!

It's time to engage in a fire-dance with the commissaires. You might get burned with a sanction, but it's worth the risk because you may just get away with it. The secret is: Don't push it. If you don't make it *too* obvious, a blind eye will be turned. Go heavy, and you *will* be sanctioned. It's a risky business. So good luck, everybody . . . and here we go.

PHASE 1: THE MAGIC SPANNER

The mechanic is now back in the car. He's had his full body moment in front of the cameras. Now it's time to go hang just half of his fine figure out of the car's right rear window.

The rider drifts over as the car pulls up alongside. Our mechanic, belly now folded over the open rear window frame, checks one of two things: the seat stem or the rear brakes. The giveaway is that if it was a front wheel puncture, there is no need to check the rear brakes or adjust for 'rub' on the rim. Anyway, out comes the magic spanner and an 'adjust' takes place while the driver of the car hits the accelerator. While the mechanic's hands are on the bike, the cyclist is magically propelled forward at pace via automotive assistance, to regain time lost due to a racing incident.

- Giveaway: Front wheel change and a rear brake check.

- Top tip: Front wheel change? Adjust the saddle stem only.

PHASE 2: THE STICKY BOTTLE

Obviously, due in part to the stress of having a puncture, it is time for a drink. It is amazing how thirsty riders get on climbs! Any uphill section clearly generates a mighty thirst. Time to go to the left-hand side of the car and take a bottle. These bottles have an amazing magnetic quality. As soon as the riders' hands touch them, the magnetism begins. Their grip, and those of the car drivers, resemble that of an electrician who's got it wrong! They both hold on for dear life as the accelerator is hit again. Only when 55km/h (34mph) is reached on a 20% climb does the vice-like grip of the car driver release, leaving the rider free to cage the bottle. I've always pondered this law of cycling physics.

- Giveaway: On release, the rider immediately chucks the full bottle into a hedge.

- Top tip: Take at least one swig before launching it.

PHASE 3: DRAFTING

'He's back in the cars,' goes the commentary call. . . meaning he's made it to the line of team vehicles sitting behind the peloton. Crisis nearly over. There is just one last piece of this dance of distraction with the race authorities: auto-assist. Get your arse as close to the bumper of every single car in the line of support vehicles as you can. Take them one by one as you move seamlessly towards the back of the pack of riders you were so unreasonably separated from through no fault of your own.

- Giveaway: Getting too close to a car and actually freewheeling.

- Top tip: Become animated. Hurl a few insults at the car in front of you as if the vehicle is actually holding you up. Use your arms in a rather flamboyant Italian way. This can help.

BLACK AND WHITE – OR GREY?

Boundaries are strange things. They are markers of the acceptable. Going beyond these will draw scrutiny at best and a ban at worst. But boundaries are there to be approached and the movement of these lines can indeed come if – and only if – it is seen to benefit the sport. Clearly, taking a train is one thing and developing a cheeky skinsuit is entirely another. Strange that, for some, this all falls within a single category: cheating.

The fact is that some teams have enjoyed a great deal of success. This makes them a target for scrutiny, and a certain false equivalence pops up. Fans and journalists who support teams that regularly get beaten cry foul too readily. Cycling so often appears to be a sport full of malcontents. I wonder if this is because in this sport it could be said there are 175 'losers' in a race and just one winner. That is a lot of bitterness right there.

Speaking to an Italian journalist, I once asked why the home fans are so forgiving of the likes of Marco Pantani and other alleged drugs cheats. He said the public view went like this: 'So he took a few potions to light up the world for us. So what? He did it for us, not for himself.' It's a tainted view, of course. A boundary crossed, sometimes with tragic consequences.

Rules to combat cheating were established in 1905, as you have learned. Sixty years later, the first detailed anti-doping laws were adopted. Since then, those who run cycling have had to keep pace with a sport playing on the edge of the acceptable in terms of technology and medicine. Currently the Therapeutic Use Exemption (TUE) rules are proving almost impossible to fathom in terms of where the boundary lies. These rules allow certain drugs to be used for therapeutic reasons, such as for the treatment of asthma. There is a limit, though. Take too much, and you are going to be punished. But when and how severely? It seems nobody knows.

The situation means that teams are almost duty-bound to push the limits of what is acceptable. Some of these actions are allowed while others are rejected and punished. The fact remains that cycling is about winning, and to win you have to dance along a line that defines the acceptable. Step over it, and you are in trouble. But the search for the boundary goes on.

17
THERE IS NO MONEY!

A few years ago, a wealthy Russian businessman, one Oleg Tinkov, decided that he was going to change the financial model of professional cycling from the inside. First he had to buy a team. He did so at the end of 2013, to create Tinkoff–Saxo, and began to stack it with massive stars like Alberto Contador, then a five-time Grand Tour winner, and Peter Sagan, soon to become a multiple World Champion. After sinking several million euros into his team, he set about working out how he was going to get his money back – and more.

His plan was to kick in the door of cycling – and ASO, organisers of the Tour de France, in particular. He was then going to take over the big pot of money and share it out among the teams and cut down the share controlled by the race organisers. But, after inviting himself to the party, he discovered that in fact there was no money. What he found out was that organisations like ASO in France and RCS Sport in Italy operate to modest profit levels. They see themselves as historic institutions and the guardians of cycling's heritage. There is not as much money in cycling as many people think.

The Tour de France is what Général de Gaulle called Un Grand Projet. He once said that if France was not engaged in a project of major global significance, the nation would retire to the cafés in a state of malaise while questioning the ranking of the first republic in the world order.

So merci beaucoup, Général, for at least defining the idea of a truly global event, but also ensuring that what Le Tour actually gets, more than any other race, is a whole lot of government support.

While some races are limited or even crippled by the cost of security, the Tour de France has none to pay. The cost of policing and road closures is covered by national and regional government. It's accounted for in local taxes as a cultural event. Want Paris closed in the centre with grandstands laid on by the Mairie? Pas de problème. Need a subsidised helicopter or five? Pourquoi pas? Paid for by the Ministry of Tourism. And do you need a dedicated motorcycle police fleet? Avec plaisir. All of these are not low cost items on a Grand Tour shopping list. In fact, without the subsidy, the Tour would resemble . . . well . . . the Giro. The Grand Tours in Italy and Spain do indeed get support, but this is modest in comparison.

What the Tour de France gets is unequivocal national support. *Everyone* in France is into it. OK, the odd nutter isn't, but everyone is certainly aware it's going on. This is not the sense one gets with either the Giro or Vuelta. A perfect example is that residents of Rome regard the Giro as a Milanese event, which is why the city only occasionally closes its streets for the 'nuisance' that is supposedly the national tour. Rome and other cities have far more important things to be getting on with than some other city's event, grazie mille. Italy, as you can tell, remains a bit divided. As for Spain and La Vuelta? Well, Spain is just plain skint. End of.

So what Tinkov thought of as a monster organisation in the form of the ASO was in fact the conduit for the French government to put on a national show. This wasn't some financial leviathan that could be leveraged into paying teams more of the TV rights. There was, and remains, no big money chest in the Paris HQ. Cycling is not a rich sport.

Tinkoff wasn't the first cycling team to close shop – as it did in November 2016 – and it certainly won't be the last. IAM went the same year and more recently Garmin had to appeal to crowdfunding to stay afloat, until Education First stepped in as a sponsor. It's tough out there. Even Team Sky declared 2019 its final season before a sponsor change. Partially a sense of 'job done', I suspect, but the huge cost of maintaining the super team must have been a consideration. Team Ineos is the new incarnation.

So how come the most watched sporting event of the year – namely, the Tour de France – makes so little money? Well, there are no stadiums. Our Maracaná or Camp Nou is a mountain roadside: the Tourmalet, Alpe d'Huez or Mont Ventoux. These are public places free to anyone who cares to turn up in a campervan with a stale baguette and bottle of plonk. No one pays to watch road cycling, least of all the Grand Tours.

It only takes one sponsor to pull out, and the team's budget is suddenly a few million short. Sponsors only put money into a team to get media exposure and their advertising budgets may change from year to year, meaning that cycling teams lead a precarious existence.

Star riders like Chris Froome and Peter Sagan make millions, but you don't have to go very far down the professional peloton before the salaries tail off dramatically.

A domestique in the Grand Tours will earn a decent enough salary to live off and have a bit left over at the end of his career to set him up in a new profession after retirement, but you only have to go down one level to pro-continental to find that isn't the case at all.

In 2018 the P&P World Cycling Revival Festival put on three days of racing at the Herne Hill Velodrome, an iconic venue that hosted the 1948 Olympic Games. One of the races was an invitational Brompton race featuring stars like ex-Grand Tour rider David Millar, and a selection of UK-based professional riders from teams like JLT Condor and Specialized-Rocket Espresso. They were racing for a Winner Takes All prize fund of £10,048.

What should have been a light-hearted affair, of decent riders chasing each other around a velodrome on fold-up bikes, turned into one of the most hard fought and competitive races of the season. The riding was fierce with the inevitable crashes, grazed skin and even broken bones. The reason? This was the greatest amount of prize money most of these riders had ever raced for. Let there be no doubt: riding bikes for a living is very tough financially.

Matt Stephens, my friend and co-commentator, is an incredible character who combined a professional racing career with another as a police officer. His first taste of professional cycling came as a youngster when he joined French team Athletic Club de Boulogne-Billancourt in the 1980s. The club remains widely respected; indeed, five times Tour winner Jacques Anquetil was a member. That didn't mean it was an easy ride for any one of the many Foreign Legionnaires who rode for them, among them Stephen Roche, Rob Millar, Sean Yates, and his 'cellmate' Jaan Kirsipuu. They lodged in a former police station.

Matt had been very excited when told that his salary was enough to live on. In fact, it was about £25 a week, which, even back then, was way less than the minimum wage. He could barely afford to buy enough food. There had to be a way of surviving. One of the tips passed around the ex-pats was to hang around when the local markets packed up at the end of the day, then scrounge around for discarded or bruised fruit and veg. This helped to cheer up the pasta meals they made themselves.

Training, racing and resting was the mantra. It was his life triangle. Matt never went out partying and barely ever had a beer.

In cycling, most of the prize money won at races is paid out to teams only at the end of the season. This allows for any fines to be deducted. So it's difficult to rely on this to supplement your income. The exception to this rule are primes (rhymes with *teams*), which are the prizes handed out for intermediate minor sprints within a race.

Matt was starving and knew his energy levels were best suited to the mid-section of a race. This was where he had a chance to win food money. As a result, he became the King of the Primes. He was always in the early break. He figured: 'Have a break, have a Kit Kat' . . . literally.

To give you an indication of how small these amounts of money can be, Sean Kelly and I were amazed in 2015 when we checked what the prize was for placing third at an intermediate sprint on a stage of the Vuelta a España. €30.

So Matt survived and contented himself each night with the thought of his share of the team's prize money due at the end of the season. Surely it would be a nice little bulging envelope; the team were going OK. Payday duly came – and the word was the bonus sum was around £3,000 per rider for the season. Matt was handed a rather thin-looking brown pay packet that was stapled to a much larger bill. 'A bill?' Mais oui!

Matt's bill was a long one. After fines there was a long list of kit he'd used. This even included spent tyres and inner tubes. 'They made me pay for every bleedin' puncture!' Deductions were £1,800. Totally deflated, he received a paltry £1,200 for his season's work. I asked Matt if that was a nadir in terms of winnings. 'No. I once won a lettuce for coming third in a race in Norfolk. There wasn't even a podium. We used a stepladder for that. The winner balanced on top, one in the middle and me on the ground . . . with my lettuce!'

I guess that's when the Cheshire Constabulary beckoned to earn a real living. He did, of course, go on to become British Road Champion and now has a successful career as a broadcaster.

Even some of those closer to the top of the cycling food chain can struggle. I was talking to a well-known Monument winner who began his career in Belgium: he rose through the ranks and was getting some handy results at Belgian Cup races like Le Samyn and Nokere Koerse. He was on the verge of breaking into the top league and well regarded in the press. However, like Matt, he had to find ways to supplement his meagre income. A big-framed chap, he needed feeding beyond the limits of his team's catering budget. What to do? The answer lay in kermesse races.

Belgium is famous for its kermesses. These are criterium-style races on a circuit around a small town or series of twinned villages. They are hugely popular, very much at the heart of grass roots, old school racing. The locals support them enthusiastically. These events are also big on 'informal betting'. Informal – as in unlicensed – local bookies set themselves up in a café at the heart of the course with a leather suitcase full of cash and a chalkboard. It's great fun.

Importantly, kermesse races offer prize money that can be taken home on the day. Good riders can pull in quite a fund from these events. Some may even get appearance money. There are also other ways of making a living on the day.

With all the unofficial betting that's going on at these events, it's unsurprising that some of the bookies have been known to get involved in massaging the results. For this, they pay good money. Imagine the scene as a cigar-munching bookie sidles up to our hungry young gun.

'I can help you here, but I need you to do something for me. I need you to come third. Not first. Not second. But third. Understand?'

Payment already delivered, it was vital for our friend to get in the day's breakaway. Once there, the real money poured in. Being in a break and the clear favourite, as he was, meant he had a sellable position. Negotiations began in earnest with those up front.

Our man simply pointed out that he could win the race hands down but was willing to ease off to let the other two go first and second – for a fee. Discussions ensued between the riders and their team cars, after which they came back to him to say that yep, they'd pay him to throw it. After a couple more visits to the team car, the bargaining finally settled on an acceptable fee. Double Double Bubble, you might say: the bookie paid him, so did the teams of the two riders who finished first and second. There was also a prize for finishing third and the original appearance money. Nice!

There are apparently more than 60,000 footballers who earn over €300,000 a year. There are fewer than 500 cyclists who can claim this. There are a handful of super-earners who make cycling a sport of princes – while those on the lowest rung of the ladder are the paupers doing all that they can just to survive.

The system doesn't exist for the riders but for the teams themselves. Riders are part of the business model. And as with all models, some of them are not attractive at all.

There is a spectrum here. At one end you have the likes of Team Ineos, super-business-like and super-funded. At the other? Enter one Gianni Savio, known as the Little Prince.

With a dapper moustache, tailored suits and a diminutive frame, this Italian team owner/manager hasn't earned that moniker for nothing. He's also the ultimate survivor and fixer in world cycling, and succeeds in finding money where there just shouldn't be any.

One way of keeping the ship afloat is to find sponsorship. And in Savio's case it seems just about anybody can join the fun. For a fee.

His team, Androni Giocattoli, has had more sponsors than just about the entire peloton put together. It has existed under various banners for the last 30 years, the one constant being that it has always had Gianni, a former football agent, at its helm.

In 2012 there were so many sponsors of the team that the actual name was Androni Giocattoli Serramenti PVC Diquigiovanni. On TV graphics they always abbreviate the team name to just three letters, which proved something of a problem. In the end they just went with AND. This represented Androni, of course, but it could also have been shorthand for the link between the five main sponsors Androni and . . . and . . . and.

With so many sponsors, the riders' jerseys looked terrible. A white background with almost every square centimetre featuring the logos of the main sponsors and secondary sponsors. From a distance, it looked like a bad pizza. It's not much better today.

Still, all those sponsors must be well pleased by his team's efforts. It's a magical mix of fading European stars and South American super-kids – all cheap to hire, they get themselves into just about every break going. And sometimes, just sometimes, it seems that Savio might pull off a big trick. Stage 18 of Giro 101 saw Mattia Cattaneo come agonisingly close to a win. He finished third that day on the big ramps up to Prato Nevoso. Maximilian Schachmann won ahead of Ruben Plaza, but the entire commentary team, from all nations, wanted it to be the Androni man.

Gianni's boy came very close. His team did eventually secure the minor prizes of the Fuga Pinarello for spending most kilometres in the break and also won the Intermediate Sprints competition. But a stage win on a Grand Tour would have been amazing.

Rightly or wrongly, Savio's team has been linked to or implicated in many dark arts. But he still comes up smiling through a set of teeth that look like he snacks on dark-roasted coffee beans. It's the only thing about him that is not polished. The cameras love him too. Like a Mafia Don, he says very few words when he nods approvingly towards one of his breakaway men – but that's enough to draw both the attention of the TV director and an extra effort from his riders.

Maybe if he looked less rakish, people would feel differently about him. But to me he represents the other side of the coin of the Team Skys, Movistars and Bahrain Meridas with their apparently bottomless bank accounts.

I'm glad that cycling has him. Without sanctioning any naughtiness here, the fact remains that Gianni has to battle to keep his team alive. It's how it always was and indeed how it remains for most of the smaller teams. As you now know: there isn't a lot of money in cycling. The only lolly you'll find easily is likely to be thrown from a publicity caravan with the name Chupa Chups written on it.

18
BACK ON THE ROAD

It's ironic, but when we're covering a bike race like the Tour de France, Giro d'Italia or Vuelta a España, we rarely, if ever, get to sit in the saddle of a bike. When we're not actually commentating, most of our time is spent either desperately trying to get some sleep or driving from one finish town to the next. We will cover literally tens of thousands of kilometres in a Skoda Estate car hired out to Eurosport and stuffed with, at times, four presenters and all their accompanying luggage and bulging egos. For various reasons the long journeys are enormous and even the shorter ones seem to get longer as the personalities in the car start to rub.

Leaving the commentary position at the end of the day's racing, Sean will lead the charge, barging past or cleverly dodging numerous people trying to get an interview or comment from him. As he races down the side streets through the crowds looking for the parked car, I'm trying to keep sight of his calves. They are easy to spot in a crowd because:

1. They're massive; and 2. They have a ginger miasma surrounding them, which lights up in the sunshine like jiggling beacons. Kelly stopped shaving his legs on retirement. 'Not doing that bloody nonsense any more . . .'

Jogging along without apparently breathing is the fitter, younger half of the Grand Tour lead team, Rob Hatch. He does shave his legs. And they are impressive. So is his agility. He glides through the fans and crew with such ease it's like he's invented a new art form: Crowd Parkour. So eel-like is his progress that he even has time to stop and chat to any number of members of the cycling caravan and pass a few bon mots in their chosen tongue. Rob is a linguistic wizard. I usually heave into view just as Rob is bidding his latest farewell and bouncing off again. I manage a wave and a panted 'Hi' to whoever he's been chatting to before battling on in search of Kelly's calves and, ultimately, the car.

At the car, I swig heartily on a bottle of the Dead Stuff: the worst-tasting of all water provided by the race. It's like previously boiled kettle water. Far fresher than I and already busy on the back seat, Rob is still in terrier mode, uploading stuff and translating press releases in exotic languages. Referring to his last stop on his run to the car, I venture: 'Who the hell needs to learn Dutch anyway? They all speak English, FFS.' 'Aaah, it's fun!' he says without looking up as he furiously types on the web. I bet he's working on Swahili at the moment. Just for fun, obvs.

If it's been a hot day – and we get some scorchers on the Tour – we have to wait for the car to cool down before departure. Doors wide open and the engine running with the air con blasting away. Not very eco I know, but needs must. We need to be reasonably comfy ahead of, say, a three-hour drive to the hotel.

So once Sean is able to touch the gear knob we chuck everything into the back and begin negotiating with race security for an exit from the parking zone. Finally the drive begins.

I always pray that Kelly doesn't have his famous 'taste for the race' as he calls it. If it's been a punchy and quick kind of a day, one that would have suited him as a bike racer, then he's at his worst – or, in his eyes, his best.

'Can you slow down, Sean?'

'Why? What's wrong with my driving?'

'Well, to put it bluntly, it's absolutely shit; you're taking far too many risks simply to keep up with the Germans. Pack it in!'

All the while, we have been taking blind corners and hill crests in Sean's mission to keep 'The Germans' in sight: former French Champion, and one-time teammate of Sean's, Jean-Claude Leclercq, who is actually Swiss and speaks German, and his colleague Karsten Migels. The unwritten rule is that the first team to get to the hotel has first dibs on the rooms.

So it's a race.

This situation is a red rag to one of the most competitive pro-racers there ever was. Sean has a Porsche 911 at home. 'Worst bloody investment I ever made. I'm too busy to drive the thing.' Trouble is, he's now pushing our overladen Skoda to the limits of its grip simply to keep up with Jean-Claude.

Probably the most annoying thing about this whole affair is the running commentary from the back seat. Rob Hatch is a vocal enthusiast given to involuntary outbursts of appreciation regarding things he loves. This applies to cycling greats in particular. Sometimes it gets the better of him, particularly where Sean is concerned, and so the encouragement to go for gaps that do not exist on a public road is both loud and frenzied. His favourite word is '*Flickage!!!*', derived from the widely used cycling term *flick*. It's a very common term in pro ranks and is used by most riders, particularly those who've spent any time in the Ardennes. 'So I flicked him' is almost a mantra when recounting any story of a win. It can be slightly derogatory as well. A bit like dispatching a bogie. It infers superiority when you do it yourself – or it can add a sense of injustice as you recall an unfair move you've suffered, as in: 'He just flicked me.' Rob has moved this on and added a little Franglais as polish. So, as Sean is divebombing lines of traffic into blind corners just for fun, and I am busy being terrified in the passenger seat, all that's audible above squealing tyres and yawing engine is Rob shouting 'Flickaaage' in the manner of an extended 'Olé' from a crowd at a bullfight. What is particularly galling is that Rob Hatch doesn't drive, so his knowledge of car handling is approaching zero. His egging-on of the nutter in control, who is now operating under a green mist, simply adds to my real and palpable sense of danger.

'PACK IT IN, YOU ARE SCARING THE SHIT OUT OF ME,' I scream. This admission of weakness, or rather fear, is a convenient get-out for Sean. It allows him to ease off without being seen to back down under orders from a lesser being.

'Ooooh. Right. Well, if you're scared, I'll knock it off a bit.'

Rob Hatch is disappointed in the rear: 'Come on Sean, don't listen.'

I rip in: 'I have got a wife and kids and I would quite like to see them again, if you don't mind.'

We drive on in silence save for Rob, who is now trying to smooth over the cracks of a parental bust-up with light chit-chat. 'Look at the colour of those shutters . . . lovely.' As he witters on about anything and nothing, I sit in silence, staring out of the window. There are still two hours of this trip to go before we reach our hotel. The air that fizzed with adrenaline now settles into a post-row stupor with a series of platitudes breaking the monotony.

'Mint?'

'Cheers.'

'THIS IS THE KANARIEBERG, AND THEY'RE NOT SINGING I CAN TELL YOU.'

Some of the long transfers are enormous – we once had to get from Normandy to Bordeaux, a hell of a drive, I can tell you. It's 650km (400 miles) and should take up to six hours. No wonder that Sean Kelly actually let me drive. But not before he'd had his fun along the way. Just the two of us in the car that day, and each time I nodded off in the passenger seat he would dab the brake to force my head to loll forward and bounce me awake.

'Pwah! Everything OK?' I would ask with a start.

'Alright,' he would say and slowly but surely I would nod off again, only for Kelly to go for it again about five minutes later.

'Pwah! What was that?'

'Rabbit,' he would say with a stony face but twinkling eyes. I realised something was afoot and so eventually I only pretended to nod off. Sure enough, after about five minutes, he hit the brakes. I opened my eyes and stared at him.

'Are you bored, Sean? Shall I drive?'

'Game's up . . . your turn.'

Needless to say, I didn't continue the game of 'Make the idiot bob his head'. No, this was not for me. I was about to have far more fun . . . with the police.

After about an hour of my shift at the wheel, on a journey estimated to take five to six hours, I spotted a snaking line of single headlamps in the rear view mirror. Result! This was the police motorcade. And they were not hanging around.

The Tour de France has a special place in the national psyche. It is regarded as a gift to the world. The French invest in other sporting events such as the 24 hours of Le Mans and horse racing's Prix de l'Arc de Triomphe, but this is the big one. And all police assistance for the race comes from the State free of charge. This includes a dedicated corps of motorcycle cops. Apparently this is a truly elite unit; the best Motorcycle Traffic Police from all over France. Securing the route and ensuring the smooth passage of the race, they seem to be everywhere during a day's stage. And they are capable of making progress extremely quickly on board their Bleu de France BMWs.

Back to my game. Now, the thing about speed cameras is that they flash, and at night you can see their activity triggered from some distance. The ideal gap between yourself and your stool pigeon, who will take the camera 'hit' for you, is around 1km (½ mile). That way, if someone in front of you causes the cameras to activate, you have enough time to slow down and avoid a fine. If those in front of you happen to be a line of elite police bikers, with a mission to eat as many kilometres in as short a time as possible, then you can regard this as a gift. Game on!

The police don't pay speeding fines when on duty. So there I was with a by now snoring Kelly snuggled on a fully reclined passenger seat while I followed the red tail lights of my friends in blue. Maybe 20 of them.

Naturally, when I first saw the motorcade in my mirrors I slowed to the speed limit. They shot by, the lead biker hanging a leg in thanks. He had clocked the official Tour race numbers on our car, I presume. Once they had sped by at an alarming rate, it took me about 15 minutes to build my speed back up and close in to the hanging distance of 1km. I was tense but happy, gripping the steering wheel so tight I was pulling myself forward off my seat back. It got so fast I was conscious of not blinking much. My eyes may have been stinging but my mouth bore a smile.

It was surreal. Deep into the French countryside, the darkness becomes total. Streetlights and illuminated signs disappear, leaving the headlamps of your own vehicle as the only guide. Unless, of course, you are tailing a force of moto-gods.

A tunnel of light thrown forwards from my own car gave way to darkness and what looked like red fireflies up ahead of me. I could see their tail lamps dancing and shifting inside a glow bubble from their headlamps. It was so dark they looked like they were hanging in space.

Sure enough, every now and then there would be a flash from a roadside speed camera. I would slow down to pass by at the limit before powering back up to catch them. As the police never eased off, it would take me quite a while to get back on their tail. And so it went on with top speeds reaching an eye-watering number that French law forbids me from repeating. Let's just say it was very, very fast.

'Wake up, Sean, we're here!'

'No feckin' way!!!'

We were about an hour and a half early. Kelly's kip was over, but he was happy. We'd beaten the Germans to the hotel.

'WHEN YOU'RE HANGING ON BY THE SKIN OF YOUR TEETH . . . KEEP YOUR MOUTH SHUT.'

Sooner or later, over the course of the spring and summer, we're going to get ourselves into one or two scrapes – brushes with the law and the inevitable speeding fines. These usually turn up a couple of months after the event, and there's the tricky question to be answered of who was at the wheel at the time. And, because the ticket has usually got to us so late, having bounced around Eurosport International offices in Paris via a hire company, there is often very little time to resolve the issue before the fine is doubled because of late payment. Thus hasty negotiations begin at Eurosport UK as to who will take the hit. Everyone knows there's no point in phoning up Sean Kelly, who will simply refuse to pay any speeding fines. I see his point. We are expected to be on time all the time for the 25 working days of a Grand Tour. Occasionally this requires a modest manipulation of the rules of the road. With so many thousands of miles covered, there is bound to be a moment when the flash goes off and a fine is issued. Sean regards this as a corporate responsibility, not a personal one. If pushed, Sean simply threatens to refuse to drive next time. As a fine is far cheaper than paying for a Tour driver, the argument simply draws to the same conclusion each year: the company pays.

Regardless of who's driving, we have a rule that they are in charge of the stereo. The only radio station Kelly will listen to is Radio Monte Carlo for the daily sport news report. 'Music? I find it very distracting,' he says. 'It's a waste of energy listening to a load of bollocks.' So it's silence when he's at the wheel, or RMC 94.2. Dan Lloyd, on the other hand, is a complete music monkey. It's all the latest rap and dance music, and he has the infuriating habit of switching from one track to another halfway through so you never get to hear a complete song. To be honest, I hate most of the music that Dan plays apart from maybe a bit of alt-J or, rather bizarrely for him, his guilty pleasure: Richard Hawley. Whenever the rap attack gets too much, I just ask for a bit of Richard Hawley to replace whatever garbage I have been subjected to. The only thing in my opinion missing from most rap music is the letter C.

'IT'S THICK RAIN. BY THAT I MEAN SLEET.'

Coming off Ventoux one year, Sean passed the honour of driving on to me. 'You need the experience,' he said. 'You need to know what it's like getting through these crazy crowds. Here's the keys.' And he chucked them at me.

On Alpe d'Huez, not only is there the issue of getting through the spectators at the end of a stage, there are also a lot of riders who regard it very much as their territory, and any vehicle, even if it's a TV vehicle that's broadcasting pictures of them all year, can be treated with disdain. They'll knock the hell out of your car with cleated shoes and full bidons. It's incredible that any hire company allows their cars to be used for the Tour because they're guaranteed to be covered in dents and scratches by the end of it.

On this occasion we got stuck behind the publicity caravan and a giant can of Nestlé iced tea trying to get round a narrow corner. As the official evacuation backed up, one of the roadside Winnebagos decided it was time to try and join the line of priority vehicles who get to leave the crowded mountain first under escort.

The guy pushing into the line of Tour cars was not driving any old pumped-up camper van. This was the sort of vehicle that is regarded in camper circles as the Starship Enterprise. Galactic in scale, it would've dwarfed a mere tour truck twice over. It carried four motorcycles on the back and even had a garage for a small car. I speculated that the roof might have a helipad.

It clearly belonged to someone important and had been stationed halfway down the mountain as a relay for someone prepared to ride down to it from the top. Immediately we thought it had to be Oleg Tinkov's private mobile hotel/entertainment centre. Despite the rule that no unbadged vehicles are allowed to enter the official evacuation line, this behemoth clearly believed it was beyond this ruling. But we saw no reason to treat it differently to any regular camper. So began the battle of wills between me in our black Skoda Estate and the driver of the gold monster.

Sean, with that familiar glint in his eye, was egging me on: 'You're not going to allow that, are you?'

Mr Tour Truck was convinced I would yield. But I was determined not to let Sean down. I was also driving a hire car that was already up to the limit of damage liability. There must have been €300 of scratches and dents on it already!

The last straw was when Mr Tour Truck let go all his airbrakes and lunged forward. It was a big move – but he didn't follow through. He immediately slammed the brakes back on, sending the truck's nose into a bobbing frenzy as the air suspension tried to cope with the now halting mass. This kangaroo manoeuvre raised the stakes. I went all in. The scratching sound still echoes in my mind.

So close were we to the truck that our wing mirror was now squashed flush with our bodywork. As I hit the accelerator it dragged itself along the side of his cab, fashioning a neat fold in the golden metal that ran about a metre in length and probably dented to a depth of 2cm. This was proper damage.

Mr Tour Truck now took a mental trip to the dark side and, for the only time I can remember, Sean looked worried. 'Oh dear, he does not look happy at all!'

The still heavy traffic meant that we had been able to move only around 30m (100ft) down the road. We watched the driver climb down from his cab. A huge gorilla of a man, he inspected the damage and duly began leaping up and down like a cartoon troll. As you'd expect, the road was rammed with security, and several officers were busy restraining our friend from paying us a visit. It wasn't long before we got the dreaded tap on the window.

The Tour Police are renowned for their no-nonsense behaviour towards anyone, particularly wayward media folk. We were in big trouble. There was a real possibility we would now lose our accreditation badges – a royal pain in the arse. If they had reached in and ripped them from the quick-release clips around our necks, we would have had to fly hastily home to continue the commentary from London off tube. Luckily, Sean's reputation goes before him. Seeing Sean, the sergeant gave us a simple Gallic wag of the finger and a fierce 'Non!' We felt like naughty school kids and responded with a whimpering 'Excusons-nous, monsieur'. We moved off slowly, leaving our still gesticulating friend and his newly resculpted multi-million-pound machine to the cops and an inevitably costly high-end respray.

'JUNGELS THERE, TONGUE OUT LIKE A SPANIEL ON A MOTORWAY.'

Sean's driving may have its disadvantages, but I'm happy on the whole to pass on the responsibility to him. He has his ways and for the most part he is good company in a sort of peaceful partner kind of way. We are like an old married couple. There is not much action but a good deal of respect and warmth. There are some oddities, though: one is that Sean is convinced that it's possible to get a suntan through a car's glass windows. He regularly displays his silverback credentials by stripping off while driving to achieve the desired bronzage. So far, his pale Irish complexion is a testament to him being completely wrong. I can also confirm that Sean has a great deal of hair, and not just on top of his head. When that shirt comes off it's like there are two of him: the inner man and the satellite miasma of deep fuzz that surrounds him. Maybe I'm wrong and it's that silvery outer shield, not the glass, preventing the tan.

CATSO!

I love Italy. Out of all the countries we visit, its mountains, coastline, olive groves and vineyards, not to mention its depth of history, never cease to amaze me. It's incredible that every part of the Tuscan landscape has been shaped by civilisation over thousands of years. There is no part of it that does not show the touch of human hands, yet it retains a majestic, almost supernatural beauty. So, a stunning, gorgeous country. Unfortunately, it's blighted by some of the most terrifying and dangerous drivers in the world.

The closest I came to death on its roads was when I was covering the Giro with Dan Lloyd. He was driving and had entered into one of those silly lane wars with another car where two carriageways narrow down to one.

The other car was a brand-new, blacked-out Porsche Cayenne Turbo. It was getting closer and closer and closer, and the guy was clearly getting angry as both he and Dan refused to give the other any space.

'Knock it off, Dan,' I said. 'He doesn't drive that thing round here from selling olive oil. The guy's f--king dangerous, can you just let him go?'

Dan thought about it, thought about it again, then said, 'No. I'm not having it.' A gap opened up and he shot into it before the Porsche could react. I looked behind and saw the driver reaching across to pick something up. It was probably just his mobile, but I was imagining something far more sinister. We were in deepest Sicily, and in that part of the world there are different rules for the sort of people who can afford to drive a Porsche Cayenne. And those rules are usually written by them. The traffic suddenly cleared and Dan floored it, Mr Corleone chasing after us in close pursuit.

However much damage this chap was about to inflict on us, either physical or mechanical, the chances were that, despite our car's Giro d'Italia livery, he'd get away with it. We screamed down the road, our Skoda Estate giving everything it had to save our lives, bless it.

Now, I cover motorsport as well as cycling. I have been driven by the greats of endurance racing and rallying. Most people, including Dan Lloyd, mistakenly imagine that they are close to elite level drivers. They are not. But what followed were some of the most skilful pieces of defensive driving I've ever seen.

Weaving through the heavy traffic, we entered a roundabout at full speed. Dan flicked the indicator and headed for a ramped exit that went down to the motorway. We must have been travelling at over 100km/h

(60mph) with our friend almost glued to our bumper. Then, at the very last moment, Dan pulled hard on the steering wheel, careering us away from the exit, our squealing and plumes of smoke rolling away in the breeze. Our pursuer reacted too late and found himself halfway down the ramp with a queue of cars now behind him. He was unable to back up. He leapt out of the car to hurl abuse at us. More than this, I swear to this day he was waving a handgun at us. No shots were fired, but the message was clear. This was very scary.

That night we were out of Sicily, many miles away from our road rage incident, but we still parked the car in a hidden corner at the back of the hotel. Just in case.

GETTING YOUR ASHFELT

If the driving in Italy is frightening, the roads themselves don't always fare any better. There's a lot of corruption, and contractors often cut corners to siphon off funding. The road may look okay as soon as it's finished, but in certain areas, usually in the south, those who have 'won' the contract have failed to lay down deep enough foundations. Any road is only as good as its underbelly. It might look fine on top, but the main cost of constructing a highway lies underground. Once the mayor has had his picture taken and cut the ribbon, the sorry story of corruption is often just beginning. The road can quickly degrade and even become downright dangerous.

Dan Lloyd and I often pass by sorry, mouldering towers of an uncompleted viaduct long past its completion date, clearly standing as a monument to corruption and ineptitude. There are regular road slips where a mountain route has simply fallen away. Some landslips are more serious than others, so Dan and I have a debate when we come across yet another Road Closed sign. Do we take a significant detour and add more time to our journey or simply go for it? We usually give it a go. The wisdom of this is highly questionable, but both Dan and I like a bet and sometimes we agree it's worth a punt.

On one occasion we came around a mountain hairpin to find a huge scoop missing from the road. It looked as if a giant had taken a snack on the tarmac. The other half of the road was intact. 'What do you think?' asked Dan. 'Er . . .' Going through my mind was the alternative of a 40km (25-mile) loop around the hill we were attempting to cross. This fact far outweighed any sense of danger on what looked like a perfectly serviceable half of road. 'Go for it, but don't hang around,' I said. We backed up about 20m (65ft) and lit up the wheels. We shot over without a problem, save for a muffled rumble behind. Our route immediately looped around to the other side of the ravine, so we were able to look back across to where we had just passed. 'F--k!!!' said Dan in a higher pitch than normal. It was a bloody miracle we'd got over. Earth and rubble was still falling from under what was now the wafer-thin strip of tarmac that remained. It looked like a magic carpet slightly buckling at the edge and hanging in the air. We were clearly the last beings who would make it over. Even a pedestrian would have brought what remained crashing down some 80m (260ft) to the valley floor. We didn't say much more to each other that night.

But the most spectacular decision to plough on regardless happened outside Naples, where our satnav had a nervous breakdown. Dan was delighted that our escape from a bowl-like finish zone had beaten the suckers queuing to escape on the official evacuation. While they grumbled in traffic, we were flying up a reasonably good-looking road that no one else seemed to know about. Merrily we pushed on as Dan mentioned how weird it was that this road was not on the satnav. We soon found out why.

The sight that greeted us was truly weird: what can only be described as a rucked-up tarmac carpet. The road had literally slipped back down the mountain and piled up in a multitude of folds at the foot. We stared at it a while and figured that if we pushed on over the mound we could then crest the peak and see what lay ahead. It might get better on the other side.

Bouncing our poor Fiat 500L over the messy bit, we pushed on over the rough foundations until we reached the top, where we were pleased to find a road surface heading down the other side that appeared good. On we went.

The Italian government is said to spend precisely the same amount of money per capita on infrastructure in all its regions. The way this money is spent, or goes missing, varies dramatically throughout the nation. The Italian Tyrol in the north is like visiting Germany; everything is clean and works perfectly. Trains, trams, roads, bridges, lighting, you name it – are all impressive. Then you begin heading south – and the further you go, the worse it gets.

So there we are, heading down from the top of the mountain. What we discovered when our car limped into the village down in the valley ahead was that we had just experienced the mess of a dual contract. Two villages were each given funding to build the road. The authorities divided the money so that contractors from each district would be employed. All they had to do was build their half of the deal and meet in the middle. The village we ended up in had the task of building along the valley bottom and halfway up the slope we were on. The town we had left had funds to build up and over the top and halfway down. The two contracts would be complete when the roads met halfway down the north side of the mountain. Well, the first part of our journey clearly showed that those foundations were non-existent. The village we ended up in had done a proper job. They had dug in their road properly. So when the two parts of the road met, there was a problem. One half differed in height from the other by a margin of around 1.25m (4ft). I know this because we got airborne where the roads met.

Dan Lloyd is a decent driver and, I have to add, a half decent pilot. If time stood still as we sailed through the air, it went even slower when the nose of the car slid a full 20m (65ft) along the surface at perhaps 65km/h (40mph) with no wheels in contact with the ground. How we didn't flip over, I will never know. During what must have looked like a remarkably well-delivered stunt, we each uttered a different but equally short word, drawing both out into very long words due to sheer terror. My *S--T!!!!!* merged with Dan's *F--K!!!!!* We now knew why this road was never opened.

'THIS TRIO OF PAIRS.'

During the 2016 Tour, the organisers, in their wisdom, decided to evacuate the whole shebang from the top of a mountain through an enormous borehole that was being constructed for a hydroelectric facility. As the cars and trucks tried to descend the steep gradient of around 25% through a dark tunnel of around 15km (9 miles) in length, Sean commented what 'total idiots' all the other drivers were. Their brake lights were ablaze. 'You'll see,' he said. 'They're using their brakes and they are going to fail. The only way down this safely is to be in your lowest gear.' Sure enough, cars started to bump into each other as the brakes wore out. It was a miracle no one was hurt. If there had been a fire, just about every TV commentator, pundit and podium girl would have been dust. The tunnel would have been a furnace chimney, for sure. We spent perhaps an hour in the choking fumes of engines, burning brake pads and toasty clutches. It was horrible. Finally emerging from the tunnel, some cars being towed out, we found ourselves behind the barrier trucks that are last to leave the race finish area and which had simply waited for the crowds to clear and make their way down the regular roads. The master evacuation plan had failed spectacularly. We were the very last to get off that cursed peak.

'A MAN THAT CAN SCARE A CAT WITH A GLANCE.'

19
AND SO TO BED – HOTEL STORIES

Those who don't 'get' me have my sympathy. They're stuck with me entering their home via their TV, a motormouth that just can't be plugged. These folk usually take to social media to tell me how I am ruining their sport and should just exit stage left and not come back – or words to that effect. And like I said, I do have some sympathy. Being comfortable in your home is a part of the right to sanity and sanctuary. One strives to be at peace and comfort in one's own space. In a busy world, we surely have a right to feel at ease for at least part of the day. So they get uppity and take to Twitter, where they find a posse of like minds ready to have a go, telling me I am but a small fish in a big pond and that I should move over to allow for a more acceptable commentator who's happy to talk time cut-off equations and minor rider career history rather than bang on about vistas, vultures and vin rouge. I get their point. But let me tell you, dear detractors, I am indeed a big fish . . . massive. And this fact unfortunately makes for some uncomfortable days indeed. Let's go to bed . . .

'Bonsoir, je m'appelle "Keer-bee". Kahh, ee, airh, bay, ee-grek.' Wait for the key. 'Un question: est-ce que un grand lit?'

The answer to the question as to whether or not I have a big bed is going to frame the rest of my stay in this particular establishment. Will it be king bed or cot? Will I have to modify the room or not? My mouth is going to turn either up or down at the edges, depending on what comes next.

'Non monsieur, un simple. Le reservation est pour un simple person.'

'Bollocks.'

'Comment?'

'Bollocks. C'est un mot anglais.'

Inevitably I am at the rear of this less than classy hotel, which, thanks to a trouser press in the lobby, sits at the top of the one-star gaffs locally. I open the door, which swings with a rusty squeak. And my shoulders drop. The musty afterglow of a thousand previous guests hangs in the air. I navigate my way along 2.5m (8ft) of brown, bubbled-up lino towards the long, thin, shuttered window, intent on airing this hovel. The room is so narrow my wheeled suitcase brushes against both the wall and my place of rest.

'This is shit,' I mumble for the umpteenth time.

I pull in the windows and push out the shutters. No burst of light, just an echo as the flimsy old wooden blinds smack the wall either side of what looks like a lift shaft to hell. It's the communal air hole to the rooms of all the poor sods who have to stay here for the night. I look up and about five floors above me I can tell there is sky, but the hanging washing of a cyclist, likewise condemned, blocks my view as a drip of water from a hand-washed sock plinks into my eye.

'This is *shit*!'

And the echo repeats . . . shit . . . shit . . . shit.

It's not all glam in the world of cycling. Just ask super-sprinter André Greipel, who suffered such terrible rooms on one Giro d'Italia night after night, he suggested it might be some form of gamesmanship.

You see, races sometimes go to rather remote locations, and this means rooms are not in plentiful supply. So basically, whoever you are, you get what's available. This can mean vast quality differences in your allotted room from one night to the next. Stars of the sport the riders may be, but on a Tuesday night in deepest Puglia that does not necessarily mean there will be many stars applied to their hotel sign. Many have none.

For me, I am not too bothered by a hotel's location. I'm not after a view. I get that all day. All I want is a bed I can turn over in without having to make what I call a 'rotisserie manoeuvre': up in the air, spin, land back down. And a bit of air con if we're in mozzie country, please. That way, if it's hot, I don't have to open the window and then get savaged. I'm convinced the reason others are not troubled by flying teeth is simply that the entire mosquito population prefers to eat me.

So I kick off my size 10 shoes, noting that end-to-end they bridge from bed to wall. There is a sink behind the slender, plywood, wobbly wardrobe at the foot of my bed. This is a small mercy as I douse a towel and drape it around my neck, in the way of a boxer, to keep moderately cooler than would otherwise be possible without air con. Lying down with my computer resting on bended knees, I try to catch up with the post-race news. Inevitably there is no internet, so I tether my phone and get on with it. The light from my computer is the only illumination. This allows me to forget the rest of the darkened room beyond my glowing bubble.

After an hour I close the laptop and let my legs slide down the bed. 'Oh for f--k's sake.'

Before the back of my knees meet the mattress, my feet hit the wardrobe, which fits precisely into the gap between the end of the bed and the sink. The bed is shorter than I am. I shout out '*Bollocks!*' so loud that I get a knock from my neighbours on either side. One shouts back 'Catso'; the other appears to have a more polite tone while grumbling something in Polish.

Thinking I just have to get on with it, I attempt to sleep in a z-form. This conciliatory mood was not, however, shared by my inner subconscious, the part occasionally given to spontaneous violence.

It was the sound of breaking glass that woke me up. That and a sense of confusion that I now appeared to have an en-suite shower. There was a knocking on the door too, accompanied by not a little concern being expressed by what turned out to be the night porter.

I flicked on the light to find my wardrobe at an angle of 45°, lying through the smashed window. To get there, it had forced the sink off the wall and the subsequent spout from the damaged pipe was now spraying the ceiling – and everything else, for that matter.

It's amazing how quickly you discover what's important to you at moments such as this. The door was thrown open by a bald guy with a pass key. Meanwhile, I was stumbling around bollock naked shouting, 'My f--king computer! Where's my f--king computer?' My friend was being equally vocal, presumably shouting something back about his bruised hotel. I couldn't tell.

I must have pushed over the wardrobe in my sleep. The flimsy quality of the unit was given to instability. Had there been a camera in the room, it would have shown a man dreaming of escape, pushing with both feet against a wall perceived to be moving inexorably his way. But it turned out I wasn't in the garbage-crusher scene from *Star Wars*; the smell was accurate, but the building not as robust. Over the wardrobe had toppled, taking the sink with it and careering through the window.

Bizarrely, the worst bit was the disdainfully accusing look I was given as the porter picked up a soggy porn mag. He held it at arm's length around shoulder height, and dropped it theatrically into the wastebasket. It was a good shot: he did this while looking directly into my eyes. I took a breath, about to explain that it must have been abandoned on top of the toppled wardrobe by a previous guest. But instead I just let out the sigh of a condemned man.

I was given another room just behind the front desk, where the porter had clearly been resting until the commotion. The next morning I got a bill.

'UP TOWARDS THE POINTY END.'

The thing about the accommodation pendulum is that it swings both ways. Occasionally you can find yourself opening a door into nirvana. For all the swings left there are those that swing just right, thank you very much.

The Milan–San Remo is a wonderful race. It's called the Primavera, suggesting the first green shoots of spring, and it marks the real start of the cycling season. It's a race longed for by fans and riders alike during a tedious winter. Say it quietly, but this is my favourite classic. Best time of year in the best country for food and optimism. It's what they do. And to this list of bests I must now add a royal bed. The King of Italy's bed, no less!

I turned up at the Hotel Globo to see three stars on the wall by the gate. A step up, I thought.

'Rather nice,' proffered Daniel Lloyd, who was with me for this one. As an ex-pro, Dan recognised a winning ticket in this game of Hotel Lucky Dip. Arriving optimistically at the front desk, we slid over our passports, which are always demanded in Italy. 'You can collect them in the morning,' said a heavily tattooed manager. Dan asked if he could have his back sooner.

'No, sir' was the *don't mess with me* reply from a rather superior man whose attitude didn't quite match his body art.

'Have I got a double bed?' I asked. The guy issued the muffled chuckle of a man in the know. His shoulders hunched and jiggled silently as he turned to get the key.

At this, Dan Lloyd gave one of his evil 'You're in trouble' laughs.

Experiencing schadenfreude is Dan's happiest state. 'This'll be fun,' he offered to himself, clearly enjoying my apparent misfortune and pondering the response.

'I take you to the room,' said what turned out to be the owner.

'No, I can manage,' I said.

'*No!* I take,' he barked.

I was a bit taken aback.

'Bloody hell, that's weird,' said Dan quietly to my back as I disappeared upstairs.

What followed can only be described as other-worldly. We came up against a pair of double doors. The only doors on the first floor landing, in fact. I noted the marble stairs had not given way to wood, as is normal once you leave the usually showy reception areas of small hotels.

He set down my case in front of a beautifully carved double door, stood to attention and stared at the door for a moment. It was as if he thought somebody was already inside. I waited uneasily.

'This . . . is . . . your room!' he said in a kind of 'ta-da' way as he flung open the doors.

I was speechless.

To say the setting was ornate is like describing the Venus de Milo as an armless statue. I can't do the sight justice, even now. It was amazing.

No inch of the amphitheatre was undecorated. The floor was mosaic, the walls all trompe l'oeil and gilding. Angels flew everywhere across a domed ceiling that mirrored the most ornate of Vatican cathedrals. The room was 'in the round' with an enormous circular bed, thankfully pushed off-centre to avoid looking like a sacrificial plinth. In a sop to modernity, there was a lounge area accommodating not one but three pale calf leather sofas. This was epic in both proportion and decoration. It was as if a bad set designer had been asked to create God's bedroom but went a bit heavy on the gold.

'What do you think?'

Some noises came out of my mouth, but frankly there was so much to take in I wasn't making sense. I sounded like I'd poured a whole tube of Barratt's Sherbet Fountain contents into my mouth and was now attempting to corral my thoughts into words through a mosh of fizzy froth and powder.

My host was more together: 'I leave you now, your highness,' he said.

At this, I kind of woke up: 'Sorry! Did you say "your highness"?'

'This is the King's bed. When he came here last time, before the bad days, the room look just the same. My family change nothing. Because one day he will come back. And we are ready.'

Bloody hell. A royalist Italian!

He rolled up his sleeves to reveal the full extent of his tattoos. These were loyalty markers for a man simply biding his time until the return of the Italian Royal Family in exile. I'm not into tattoos, but these were amazingly well rendered. Like fine paintings.

Pointing out their significance, he went on: 'This is the King, and this is God. They are like the same! That is how it is.' With that, he backed out of the room, gracefully grabbing both doors and bowing as he closed them symmetrically. I felt like I'd witnessed a dress rehearsal.

I was lying down dead centre of the bed in a crucifix position, contemplating the cherubim and seraphim gazing down at me, when the room phone rang.

I could tell by his tone that Dan was grinning as he enquired: ''ello mate, how's your single room?'

'Fine. How's yours?'

'Brilliant, actually. Nice view over the square, lovely big bed and bath. Couldn't be happier! Heh, heh, heh. You got a minibar?'

'Yes I have, but honestly I don't think I can be bothered to walk all the way over to it.'

'What?'

'Dan, get your arse down here.'

We stood there together in silence, looking up at the ceiling.

Eventually, Dan broke off in full attack mode. 'Right, let's go get a beer!'

Dan had been beaten in the room stakes for the first time in a long while. He hates losing at anything. It's an athlete-predator thing. So he duly declared beer o'clock to help him forget my shattering victory on this momentous Good Bed Day.

20
PARTY TIME!

Stelvio, Giro 2012.

'Porca Madonna! The light! It says we have no fuel. Shit!'

And so it was that Gianni Farina, a lovely guy but also the worst driver on Planet Earth, announced we were out of fuel in our attempt to go over the Stelvio, one of Europe's highest mountains and not exactly awash with fuel stations. 'Porca Madonna', Farina repeated.

If you ever hear this expression from an Italian, you know that he's more upset than he can possibly tell you. It is blasphemy of the highest order. The only non-Italian I ever heard say it was Chris Froome during a race in Italy. I was stunned, because he also knows the weight of it. It was directed towards someone barging him in the pack during a nervous start. My situation was more serious.

'You, my friend, are a prize pillock.'

'What is a pillock?'

'You are! I told you to fill up earlier and you told me to "chill out". How the hell are we going to get over this bleedin' mountain, you complete idiot?'

So there we were, halfway up a giant peak at an altitude that meant the temperature was around 16°C (60°F). There was a light mist falling and the night was now well installed. It was 9.30 p.m. I was fuming.

'It's OK, we turn around and we switch off the engine. We go down in neutral. Gravity you see, all is good!'

'No, all is not good at all, my friend. Without the engine running, you have no power steering and no servo brakes. At the first serious corner you will lose it and . . . *we . . . will . . . die!* Do you understand?'

'I still think we can do it!'

'*Well, I do not!* We keep going on f--king vapours and you will drop me off at the first place we find with a bloody light on. You can collect me in the morning. If, that is, you survive your downhill bobsleigh ride.'

Now, this all probably sounds a bit prima donna-ish. But honestly I was just about at the end of my thinly stretched tether. Dan Lloyd had gone off earlier with a far more capable film unit to do some background reporting on the top of the peak. So here I was, alone with my producer buddy from Rai Uno's commercial department who, it has to be said, had a rather relaxed attitude to all things logistical. Like fuel.

Earlier I had been forced to grab the steering wheel on two occasions as Farina had been distracted and the car began to drift dangerously. How this man had ever passed his driving test was beyond comprehension. He must have paid somebody to do the test for him, I speculated. Then again, how could he possibly find someone who even closely resembled him? He is spectacularly hard to describe due to the cloud of smoke that hung permanently in his midst. I'm certain that, while awake, he had never taken an adult breath free of tobacco smoke. His hobbit-like frame was shrouded in a charity shop sports jacket, clearly donated by a much bigger man many years earlier. It fitted him like a glove . . . an oven glove.

Farina was so small that there was a lot of room around him in the driver's seat. He used this space as a sort of exercise yard and constantly fidgeted in his seat. He even once sat cross-legged after setting the cruise control to 165km/h (102mph), only to go into ninja mode when a traffic jam suddenly appeared. His legs were still knotted under him until the last moment when our screaming tyres finally found purchase. The clouds of tyre smoke billowed past us as we came to rest about 1m (3ft) away from a truck's back lights. The silence in the car was broken by our lunatic chauffeur who, seeing the halted traffic extending far off into the mouth of a tunnel, observed in a matter-of-fact way, 'It was here in that tunnel I had my third big accident.'

Wide-eyed and pale as a night poacher, I was able to say only, 'Oh.'

Back on the mountain, we rounded a corner, the car just starting to splutter, and came upon a mountain lodge restaurant with a host of race vehicles parked outside. Sanctuary!

'Right, this'll do. Thank you, gentlemen.' I flounced out of the car and dragged my bag from the boot. Tapping the roof, I said, 'Off you pop! See you in the morning.'

I could hear the sound of the restaurant through the double-glazed windows. As I climbed the steps, the door flung open and a wobbling barrier guy exited, guffawing with laughter as he made his way over to a tree. He couldn't be bothered to battle for the loo through the mayhem inside. There must have been 200 covers, and not a seat was free. Production crew, barrier guys, and promotion caravan teams of all descriptions were theatrically engaged in a food festival. The mood was buoyant to say the least; rowdy even.

Doing the world television feed on-site is a privilege. You are a member of a big but tight production team and thus very much part of the gang. So they knew who I was. 'Ciao, *Carl-toni*!!!' echoed around.

I asked a harried waiter who among all his clients was about to finish? He pointed to a table of trolls. These guys needed a bath. I didn't care because they were kind, going my way over the mountain and apparently had space in the cab of their heavily laden flatbed truck stacked with hundreds of aluminium barriers. They also reflected the diverse heritage of the barrier crews, whose job it is to secure the race route with a line of shiny aluminium. My new mates were, it turned out, Italian, Slovakian and Sicilian.

Espressos necked and cigarette butts flicked, we got on board. It was tight. They said they had room, but this was clearly for the size of an arse that belonged to Farina. His arse, meanwhile, was heading down the mountain in a dance of death with hairpins and oncoming TV trucks. I didn't care.

With the smile of an escapee in sight of freedom, I wound down the window and hung an elbow into the cold air just to give my shoulders some room. There were four of us on the bench seat of the cab. We were as cosy as four grown men can be.

It's hard to pass sweets when your shoulders are compressed to the side of your face. With arms out front in a begging position, we passed around a plastic box of Tic Tacs and launched the sugar pills into our mouths as if we were tossing pancakes.

The road got progressively steeper and more broken. The municipality had not got around to fixing the winter frost damage and the truck was duly being troubled by the uneven surface. On we bounced for around 20 minutes before we rounded a headland to be met with a terrible sight: red warning flares were firing their powder into the night. It looked like an emergency chopper landing site from *Apocalypse Now*. This was serious.

Out of the hellish fog came a policeman. I imagined Verdi's *Requiem* as the smoke billowed and wafted about him as he walked towards us.

We turned our engine off to hear the fizzing fireworks as the officer drew near.

'Landslide?' I enquired sympathetically.

'No . . . no, no, no,' said the policeman with a huge grin on his face. 'Party!!!' It was then I noticed the very faint thrum of rock music. I think it was Lynyrd Skynyrd.

'You park here and walk around the big hole . . . 200m you find the party.'

'Thank you, officer.'

We found the big hole alright. Clearly a pothole that had once been covered, as we discovered, by a 5cm (2in) thick sheet of iron to accommodate rolling trucks. The bolt holes were fresh in the road. So was the air temperature as we marched on towards what looked like a Native American encampment.

A huge teepee revealed itself, located next to a massive bonfire. It was apparently still dinner time. Over the fire was an arrangement of wooden poles, from the centre of which hung the metal sheet now missing from the road. It swung gently on its chains with piles of meat on board sizzling away about a foot above the log pyre. This was mega!

I can honestly say I've never seen so many dangerous looking men gathered together in such a happy mood. 'Ciao, welcome,' said a man with a huge two-litre bottle of something boozy. 'We are the Giro Mountain Guard.' It was a Biker Gang.

Basically, if you are a mayor, in hard-pressed times, and you want extra security for a one-off event, then the Hells Angels are a handy bunch to befriend. Apparently the local police force would struggle to secure a race such as the Giro without them.

So here we were in a mosh of hairy men with lots of food, a fire to keep warm . . . oh, and alcohol. Booze-a-go-go.

'You like grappa?' said a man who resembled Father Christmas's tubby brother. He displayed a bare belly, curtained at the sides by a leather waistcoat that had buttons but no chance of them ever being fastened.

He handed me a pottery demijohn with a finger loop at the neck, from which I was clearly expected to swig. I pulled a long cork and went to take a nip. 'No, no, you drink it like this,' and he showed how to balance it on your elbow and tip it up. Under his excited gaze. I took a hearty swig. *Wow!*

Now, I have had some drinks in my time. Toddy in Tuvalu, made from coconut tree sap; Bissap in Burkina Faso, made from hibiscus flowers; Arrack in Sri Lanka, made from palm syrup; whiskies, eau de vies, and a myriad other types of firewater from all over Planet Earth. But if you put them all on a table and I had to pick just one, I would chose Italian Hells Angel Father Christmas Juice every time. It was fabulous. Smooth as you like with a donkey-kick finish.

'I made it myself,' he said proudly. 'It's delicious,' I said, handing it back. 'No, no, no. That is your bottle, we have plenty.' He gestured to a pyramid of unopened bottles stacked just yards away in the dancing shadows. 'Enjoy!'

And I did.

I don't know how I got to my hotel room that night. In fact, I don't know much about what happened after perhaps my third gulp of grappa. There is a photo somewhere of me wearing what appears to be a sun hat standing at the rear of my new band of brothers. I have my arm raised, shouting cheers towards the camera. Soon after this was taken, I must have passed into oblivion.

I awoke the next morning in a beautiful room around 30km (18 miles) away from the mountain party. As I came to, I realised I was very cold indeed. I lay spreadeagled on a king-sized bed with large French windows flung open to a modest balcony. We were facing east, so the morning sun was pouring past gently waltzing net curtains. From the bed, the view contained nothing but sky. I was clearly still at altitude. It was then I looked down to see that I was completely naked, save for one foot that still had a shoe and sock on it. Then I saw all the clothes strewn around the room. I had clearly undressed myself and performed a dance of death while trying to get my trousers off over the shoe. Luckily I'd landed on the bed instead of tipping over the balcony and down the gorge that fell away 300m (1,000ft) or so from my hotel, perched on the mountainside.

Later that morning, with dark glasses and aspirin doing a lame job on my headache, I saw my Slovakian and Sicilian friends as they unloaded their barrier truck. 'Was it you guys that took me home last night?' No words were returned. What I did get was uproarious laughter and the shaking of heads as they worked on, pouring with sweat. To this day, I still don't know how I made it to safety that night. I remain concerned that there may be a sequence of incriminating pictures awaiting release on to the internet.

'NOT TOO HOT, NOT TOO COLD, JUST LIKE THE THREE BEARS' PORRIDGE.'

21
THE GREATEST RIDE

What makes a great ride is not always as simple as winning a bike race. What truly stirs the emotions, certainly with me as a commentator, is when undiluted human endeavour is displayed in its myriad forms: fortitude, panache, bravery, doggedness, flamboyance, verve and sheer guts. Cycling has always been about going deep. And the deeper you go, the darker it can get.

Greatness isn't always accompanied by champagne and laurels. Sometimes it comes with blood and bandages. From my position as a commentator, I've had the privilege of sitting at the finish line and witnessing these extraordinary feats from a group of sportsmen that put so much of themselves into this dramatic sport.

The greatest riders have always been the ones able to suffer for longer than the rest. Think of Jacques Anquetil, Fausto Coppi, Gino Bartali. But it wasn't just innate talent that helped them win. Sure, they had that in spades, but never forget how important is sheer bloody-mindedness. It's perhaps almost the most vital strand of any successful rider's DNA.

Post race, commentators are often given to pondering great rides of the past over a beer or at dinner. As a group, we are in awe of those about whom we speak. It's a reverence. And we often drift into a mild cycling quiz, asking questions of each other. Testing. Wondering. There used to be a regular question that drifted in: 'What's the greatest ride for you, then?' In recent times, I've witnessed some remarkable rides that have had me pouring emotion from the commentary box. And they haven't all been famous victories, either.

Iljo Keisse on the Tour of Turkey 2012 led the pack into Izmir by 16 seconds at the flamme rouge. He fell on a right-hander, remounted and then dismounted again to put the chain back on. Finally on his way, he then held off big sprinters like Alessandro Petacchi and Marcel Kittel in a drag race to the line.

Think of Nairo Quintana on the Tour 2015. He was second in the general classification, behind Froome, and his do-or-die push in the Alps had me out of my seat and willing him on. First he did it on La Toussuire, then he dropped his rival again on the following stage on Alpe d'Huez. It was amazing.

Then there was Thomas De Gendt up the Stelvio Pass at the Giro in 2012, beating off Michele Scarponi by nearly a minute and coming very close to stealing the entire race.

And who can forget Steve Cummings' stage victory on the 2015 Tour, when he bridged to Romain Bardet and Thibaut Pinot on the way up to the airfield at Mende, winning on Nelson Mandela Day for the South African team MTN–Qhubeka?

These were great rides. There are many more. Some you'll find elsewhere in this book. But if you're looking for an historic ride in recent times, and possibly of all time, look no further than the Giro d'Italia on 25 May 2018 and Chris Froome's extraordinary stage victory at Bardonecchia, where his 80km (50-mile) solo break clinched the Giro. It was awesome – in the correct use of the term. I remain, as do many, simply in awe of the achievement. It will never be forgotten.

It had been a crazy race up to that point, bizarre and intriguing and full of the unexpected. To understand how Froome performed this seemingly superhuman feat, you have to understand the context and what had happened in the preceding months.

The problem with great rides is that if you do them, there are question marks, and if you don't . . . there are yet more questions. When Froome came into the Giro, half the press corps thought he shouldn't be there because of the Salbutamol case hanging over him. Many others thought he was undercooked because he would surely have to hold something back for the Tour de France.

He was damned if he did and damned if he didn't. Had he not won the Giro, everyone would have been saying, 'Aha! So he's now no longer got the stuff that won him four Grand Tours.' Then he wins and people go, 'Aha! He's still clearly taking advantage; this must be questionable.'

Froome had crashed some days earlier, while on a recce of the course for a time trial in Jerusalem. And he looked in poor form there too. At that point, my heart really went out to him. Turns out he was running himself into form, because a few days later he skipped up Monte Zoncolan like a gazelle and won the stage. The press reaction was, 'That's amazing – or is it?' The stage victory seemed to attract dark clouds of suspicion.

The next day he was dropped spectacularly and the speculation then was that he was finished, spent like a cheap firework. The focus moved on to Simon Yates, who had become the unexpected race leader. As Froome fell further behind, he seemed to be completely out of contention. His odds went down. One of my editors, Massi Adamo, asked me, 'Do you think he can come back from this?' Because he was way down, over three minutes behind in the general classification, I said, 'It's possible, but it's unlikely.' Massi put on €40 at 50-1 at that point. Then the day before the big stage – the now remarkable, historic stage – Massi doubled his money up. 'I had a dream!' he said. And of course sometimes, just sometimes, these come true.

Form is never constant. Class is, but form will waver, especially when you go deep on your approach to form, which is what Froomie was doing. He was striking a balance to enable him to defend his Tour de France title later in the year. You can overdo it, knock yourself back, go too deep too soon, just like Fabio Aru did on the same race. With Chris, it's about balancing the form – famine to enjoy the feast. Carefully does it.

When Froome set off on that stage, he'd clearly got his legs back and his team were absolutely incredible – the way that they attacked was magnificent! I was lucky enough to be calling the race that day and you could see Team Sky strategising; putting the pressure on everybody before they put the hammer down with a blistering early pace. It looked like a suicide mission. 'They're making plans,' I declared, but I admit there was an element of hope.

When Froome went off with 80km (50 miles) to go, we were thinking, he's gone shit or bust. 'Surely this is madness,' I said on air. He'd been on the radio and he apparently said, 'Come on, guys, this is it. We can do this. Let's go, go, go.' That absolute undiluted belief is the sign of a great rider, to my mind.

There were two climbs that he had to conquer, firstly the dirt track of the Finestre. It was an infernal tempo designed to hurt the likes of Tom Dumoulin. Simon Yates was dropped early and when it was down to a select few, Froome powered away. All this with the magnificent backdrop of a majestic snow-covered mountain on a gravel track that called to mind the great rides of Fausto Coppi and Gino Bartali. If it wasn't for the garish team kits and carbon bikes, you could imagine you'd been transported 60 or 70 years back in time.

If Froome's performance up the Finestre was magnificent, he was about to outdo that achievement by an extraordinary descent, where he gained most of the time he won over the Dutchman. It's incredible to think that there were once question marks about Froome's descending and bike-handling skills. That descent off the Finestre was an absolute masterclass – beyond the scale of even the very best I'd seen till then.

Of course, it's likely he was guided down by Nico Portal in the support car behind him, in the same way that a rally driver takes instructions from his co-driver. Properly researched and dialled into the mind, the instructions would've sounded like this: 'Off camber, three left . . . warning, pinch point in 300m, 200m, 100m, pinch point . . . and accelerate.' Even so, it took masterful bike craft to deliver such a descent – and he did.

The Finestre and the downhill dealt with, Froome then had to climb up to Bardonecchia, which he attacked in his familiarly awkward, high cadence, crabby style. And getting to the finish line he powered through, conscious of every second he could gain over Dumoulin. Dumoulin himself said that there was nothing more he could have done on the day: he'd given it his all and was proud of his performance despite losing over three minutes to Froome.

It was a stunning performance that also highlighted the military precision and organisation of Team Sky. Not only did his teammates put in the initial damage on the lower slopes of the Finestre, the level of planning from the management was immense. They had realised that if he was to make a break at 80km (50 miles) out, there was clearly no way he would be able to sustain the level of effort required without proper sustenance: energy bars, gels, drinks and water had to be delivered to him along the way. So it was that the entire team were deployed at key parts of the course – everyone from the swannies to the press officer to manager Dave Brailsford were on the side of the road to pass him whatever nutrition he needed, all of which had been carefully calculated the night before by the team nutritionist.

The stage win was remarkable, but the implications even more so. Victory here put him in the pink jersey, and, with only an individual time trial to come, had to all intents and purposes won him the Giro itself. He was now the holder of all three Grand Tour titles simultaneously, something that had not been achieved in the modern era.

The reaction to what should be more widely regarded as an historic victory, especially now that Froome has been vindicated over the Salbutamol case, was, sadly, mixed. The New Zealand rider George Bennett poured scorn and suspicion on the performance by saying live on TV, 'No way. He did a Landis. Jesus!' (Floyd Landis famously put in an astounding performance at the 2006 Tour de France at Morzine to win the race, only to be found positive for traces of testosterone later.) Later, Bennett was quoted in the press: 'He made a bigger comeback than Easter Sunday.'

I overheard one French commentator, who has always referred to Froome as The Kenyan, say, 'Hmmm. So the jersey passes from one asthmatic to another.' (Froome had taken the jersey off Simon Yates, a rider whose team paperwork in 2016 meant his own permitted anti-asthma treatment was not properly registered. He served a four-month suspension.)

I believe that Froome put everything into that day, drawing on all his resources – emotional, psychological, physical. He went all-in on every level. He drew on the anger and frustration of what had happened in the months leading up to it. That anger is a very big part of what drives him and always has. He got angry with Wiggins when he had to look after him in 2012. He's vicious when he needs to be. He's the ultimate predator. And this victory was the ultimate two fingers up to the press who had been hounding him constantly over the Salbutamol case. Likewise he stuck it to his opponents, fellow riders who had publicly spoken out against him racing the Giro and who now fell silent. He had rounded on his critics using his legs, spirit and formidable intelligence. It was a cathartic moment.

Personally, I feel great sympathy for Chris Froome. Every victory he achieves is received only grudgingly by press and public alike. There are always questions over his wins, and when he doesn't hit that stellar form, there are questions about that too. What does a guy have to do? It's ironic that he equips himself so politely and respectfully in public yet gets such negative press. I believe in the future, as his career is fully quantified, Froome will be treated much more kindly.

So whose was the greatest ride ever? For me, the question has a definitive answer. Froome's attack that day and subsequent stage win and ultimate Giro victory was an other-worldly performance. We won't see such a ride again. Chapeau, sir!

'IT'S CHRIS FROOME THAT WILL BE IN THE COLOMBIAN SANDWICH.'

22
THE OTHER BIKERS

There are more motorbikes following Grand Tour races than ever before. Some of them are essential to the broadcast and wider media. Some are not.

Now, I like motorbikes. I have one myself. In 1993 I completed what was known as a Super Course. I still can't believe it, but in the space of just 10 days I went from total novice to the owner of a full motorcycle licence. I was, remarkably, suddenly allowed to ride absolutely any motorcycle on sale, no matter what capacity. It was a licence to kill . . . myself.

Not surprisingly, you can no longer do such a short Super Course: the accident rate in graduates was rather high. Having riders with just 10 days' experience spanking around, potentially on superbikes, is no longer deemed wise. Surely, you are thinking, no one would be mad enough to buy a high-powered motorcycle with under two weeks of riding experience.

Er, hello?

I went from training on a 125cc Honda Plastic to being the proud owner of a Harley-Davidson FXR Evo 1,360cc Police Bike. It was madness.

I remember going along to Warr's Harley-Davidson just off the King's Road to collect my treasure. When I got there, it was standing outside the wash shop, on a back road, looking amazing. All paid up, I swung my leg over it and levelled it before setting off. It weighed a ton. I was in trouble. Suddenly I realised I was in charge of something of which I had absolutely no experience. It was like going from flying kites to a Spitfire. Sure, I had the paperwork. But nothing else, let alone a speaking voice. I was terrified.

I started her up and gently let the clutch begin to bite. Slowly I moved into the road. As I grabbed a handful of revs, the salesman came out of his office and waved. I waved back. With my clutch hand . . . *Booom! Aargh!!* The bike lunged forward and I was thrown back, forcing my only gripping hand to wind open the throttle further.

In super-slow motion, this would have looked amazing. Like something you might find on YouTube under 'Fat Ballet Biker', with the soundtrack of 'The Blue Danube' accompanying subtitles:

'This is Houston: Apollo, you are clear of the tower.'

I hurtled along, rattling windows as if I'd been shot out of a cannon. I fired past frightened kids being scooped up by mothers. 'Wanker', mouthed one.

I pulled on the brakes in panic, the machine coming to such a dramatic halt I nearly went over the handlebars. The engine stalled.

I sat there white as a sheet, panting. 'What the hell have you done, you mad arse??' I murmured.

And I had a bigger problem here: I was living in northern France at the time. So there I was, a complete novice in charge of a leviathan about to set off through London traffic, destination Dover. I was due to take a ferry bound for Calais, from where I had a further two-hour ride on country roads to my old farmhouse in Raye-sur-Authie. Twat!

I still don't know how I made it. That night I calmed myself next to the stove with a bottle of red, my left forearm swollen with carpal tunnel strain from the heavy clutch. It could have been so much worse. I spent the next two years learning to ride the thing properly around the near deserted roads of Picardy.

All of this means that I am fully conversant with the entire gamut of crap motorcycle handling, having passed through all levels of danger and idiocy my very self. I know what good and bad riding looks like. And I duly pass judgement on this regularly while commentating.

Good Bikes carry TV cameramen and photographers satiating our rapacious hunger for images, both moving and still, on all forms of media.

Bad Bikes carry fluff. These are a PR or money-making exercise and are a bloody nuisance. Sure, the head of the local yogurt factory might get a buzz out of riding with the pack. Well, get lost, Mr Milko, you're in the way!

The recent upsurge in VIP bikes is not just annoying, it's also dangerous. The riders of these bikes are not at the top of the pecking order in the squadron. So you have a lesser skilled rider coupled with an often rather unwieldy besuited businessman who's been crammed into waterproof overalls. He's the jiggling pillion passenger. It makes for an unstable presence around the peloton. And this is bad news. I wouldn't mind if there were one or two, but there are loads: I counted 12 one day! Add to that the expanded number of press and blogging media now paying for access, and you have a swarm of active vehicles on the course, which is beginning to affect the racing. I get nervous and I know the riders are too; perhaps more so.

The VIP machines at least have the excuse of inexperience. The photo boys do not. And the drive for drama on dedicated cycling blogs and social media means the hunt for an arty, 'up the nostril shot', as I call them, finds motorcycles getting closer and closer to riders who don't have the benefit of leather and body armour in the event of a collision.

'Get that bike out of there!' I often exclaim as they get too close.

I know I sound like a campaigner, and viewers are split on this. Some agree while others tell me to shut up and stick to commentating. The fact is, there have been unnecessary accidents and this has finally led to a 30m (100ft) proximity rule being adopted by some races: not mandatory just yet, but that will come.

Even the good bikes get it wrong sometimes. Descending ahead of the riders is difficult because some of the best pro cyclists will be travelling faster than the motorcycles, which are far more cumbersome to handle on a twisty descent than lightweight carbon cycles. And a professional rider desperately trying to make up time on his rivals will take more risks. So filming in front of such riders can actually hamper the racing: the riders keep catching up and are sometimes hampered by those taking pictures.

Filming from behind is even more fraught with danger. We often see riders' back wheels slip away dramatically in a curve, whether due to an unstable surface, fluid on the road, a puncture, or simply misjudging a curve. A motorcycle who's following too close could easily run a rider over. This has happened in the past.

Camera bikes are a necessity. Without live action TV pictures, cycling would die as a sport. So getting these shots is always a compromise. If only all cameramen could be Patrice Diallo.

Where there are serfs, there has to be a Duke. And that man is Patrice Diallo: the most accomplished camera motorcyclist there is. The guy is a genius.

Patrice rides like he's been on a bike since before he could walk. Which is handy because now he can barely walk, having crashed so many times when he was young. His right leg in particular looks like a madman with a cheese grater and a mallet has had some fun with him. Multiple fractures and burns have scarred him badly.

Patrice can't dance. But a motorcycle, in his hands, does. The finesse displayed by Patrice and his machine is simply remarkable. His ability to control his bike, while accounting for the added load and imbalance of a cameraman with all his kit, is remarkable.

The platform he provides for generating pictures is as stable as they come, even on a highly technical, mixed surface descent. Every cameraman wants to work with Patrice. He is so experienced he knows when and where to go, how to get there and how to get out. It's almost as if the cameraman just has to press the button because Patrice, with the lines he is taking, has set the shot up for him.

He gets through gaps clinically and safely while telegraphing his moves effectively so the riders also have absolute faith in him. He knows where he's going, so do they. That level of assurance between cyclist and motorbike rider comes from vast experience and notoriety.

I've seen Patrice on site all over the world from the Tour de France to the Tour de Langkawi in Malaysia. He's the favoured rider of Euromedia, who provide the hardware to France Television and thus Le Tour. More often than from any other ground level source, the pictures filling your screen are taken from Patrice Diallo's bike.

Don't go thinking this man is anything like a robot. He is an artist – and sometimes, out of necessity, a clown.

But it's not just bike-handling that gets the pictures. Location-finding is also part of the art. Patrice gets himself into amazing positions. He'll race on and set up a static ride-by of the main favourites, get away safely, stop safely and then get exactly the shot to surprise and entertain. In Qatar, I once saw him open a jam jar containing a live scorpion. He placed it on a rock on a bend. The cameraman was delighted. He bobbed down and did a pull-focus as the peloton cruised by. Wonderful. The menace of the heat was never better described.

Over the years, Patrice has learned many tricks to generate atmosphere. He carries two things with him at all times. A rubber red nose and a Super Soaker water pistol. Want smiling kids? Any TV director does. Problem is, the expectant fans have been waiting for hours in the baking sun and are a bit tired and fed up. Then Patrice arrives. His big round friendly sunburnt face naturally raises a smile anyway. He winks and twists the ends of his luxurious moustache before adding the touch of the red nose.

The crowd are now amused, but the shot is still not at peak jollity. Time for the coup de grâce: out comes the Super Soaker. '*Allez!*' screams Patrice and starts blasting the crowd with water. It's mayhem! The perfect warm-up act has done his job. The cameraman gets a load of geed-up fans in the sunshine and, right on cue, he pulls back to get the riders approaching. Without our friend Patrice, none of this would have happened. Good TV pictures take work. Sometimes they are fraught with danger. The best in the business make generating such images as this look easy. It is not. Ride long and safe, Patrice. We need you.

'THAT'S THE DANISH BRINGING HOME THE BACON.'

23
WHEN THE PLUG GETS PULLED

The quality of images from bike races broadcast into homes all over the world has improved dramatically in recent years. When you look back at old footage from 15 and 20 years ago, it was beset with pictures breaking up – and, at times, it was very difficult to make out who the riders were. I remember having to commentate from the back of a van with a towel over my head and a black and white monitor while I tried to decipher who the riders were from their posture because I couldn't even make out the colours of their team kit. While we're blessed by great improvements in technology that offer pin sharp images, even cameras attached to the riders' bikes, there are times that I can't stop marvelling at how it all comes together. Occasionally it doesn't.

The process involved in delivering live cycling on TV is a complex one, and it takes only a small error for the whole show to come crashing down around your ears. The pictures on your TV set at home, whether from a motorbike, a helicopter or static camera by the side of the road, have to go a circuitous route of being pinged up to a circling fixed-wing aircraft and sent back down to the outside broadcast vehicle. This truck sends the signal to a hub-transmission facility in, say, Paris if we are on the Tour. This is then sent via satellite to your provider, who mixes in commentary and retransmits the signal to its own network via either cable, internet or satellite and thus into your home. One tiny error, the smallest slip-up, will put paid to all the hard work of engineers, cameramen, directors, helicopter pilots and producers. When the live pictures fail, there is usually a play-loop of general pictures until the link is fixed. And at a moment such as this it's up to the commentator to try and plug the gap.

Remember the dream you had about standing naked in the middle of the Wembley pitch on Cup Final day? Yep, that's the feeling.

I was on the Tirreno Adriatico in 2013 where Lloydie and I were voicing the world feed, as opposed to the feed from Eurosport. Before transmission, we were inadvertently filmed for filler by a cameraman who didn't know us. We were having a spot of lunch – calamari and a glass of prosecco, I think it was. Dan and I had been joined by two colleagues: Valentina Lualdi from the organisers, RCS, and Sophie Ormond of IMG, the managing agents. We would have looked to the cameraman like a perfect pairing of two couples out for lunch in the sunshine (had I not spoiled the effect by looking like their Dad).

Anyway, it was a bit of atmos footage, shot purely as filler to set the scene at the finish line. Unbeknown to us, our guzzling faces were shortly to appear on the Eurosport broadcast, and not just a fleeting glimpse either. We were on a three-minute loop that was shown again, and again, and again. The line had failed and the only fill-in footage they had was our little luncheon.

The problem began a few hours earlier, when the broadcast technicians had set up the satellite dish that was to beam the pictures of the race to the world. The truck had been lined up and secured, the dish had been angled correctly, and Sergio and Giuseppe had dusted their hands and disappeared to the local bar to congratulate themselves on a job well done. Only, they hadn't done the job at all well. While they'd remembered to do all the big complicated stuff, there was one small thing they'd forgotten. Giuseppe had the simple task of snapping down a clip bolt that locked the dish on the roof of the truck to its satellite tracking base. He simply forgot the simple.

It was a windless, sunny day, so the dish behaved impeccably initially. Our lunch was a distant memory when the helicopter made its first pass over the truck. We were in the last hour of the stage as the loop section of the course was to begin, four times over the finish line being the plan – and most of the world didn't get to see it.

The chopper was doing a reverse heads-up shot of the peloton as they came down what would be the home straight in a few laps. He was low and the pictures were amazing. The sea was as sparkly as a cocktail dress, the palms waving and the crowd bellowing.

As the helicopter flew overhead, the downdraft blew the unsecured satellite dish a degree or two off line. The uplink was broken. All the outbound pictures went pop. Two seconds later, the backup shots went to air: Dan Lloyd, Valentina, Sophie – and Dad. You could almost hear a backing track: Summer Madness.

The producers in the broadcast truck were in a panic.

'Quick, what other pictures do we have while we get this shit sorted out?'

'Nothing else boss, sorry.'

'*Testicoli!*'

Back in London, Declan Quigley was commentating for Eurosport and, in his finest warm Irish lilt, began to describe the pictures he was seeing: 'Well, ladies and gentlemen, we apologise for the lack of footage of the race. Please bear with us while we sort this out. Ho, ho, ho.

Goodness me, take a look at what's going on down at the finish line . . . Ah, it's alright for some! That'd be Carlton Kirby and Daniel Lloyd on your screens right there, that's Carlton on the left. The, ahem, larger of the two.'

Declan naturally fully described the scene, thinking this was just a brief shot. But three minutes later, the technical problems hadn't been sorted out, so this same footage of Dan and I popping pieces of calamari in the company of our minders cropped up again . . . and again . . . and again . . .

Declan was now struggling to repaint the image for viewers: 'I wonder what they're eating? Have you any idea, Brian? Pasta, perhaps?'

Brian Smith, in his *Hey mate, this is your problem, don't get me involved in such flimflam* kind of way, simply said: 'Yeah, could be,' and it was back to Declan. You can't usually hear a man sweating. You could on this day.

Simple as the fault was, it could not be found. All client broadcasters, including Eurosport, finally took mercy on their viewers and commentators and duly pulled the plug.

The dislodged dish was used to relay pictures away from on-site. For Dan and me, there was no picture loss, so we continued our commentary, all of which was used in the highlights show later. Naturally, out came the internet trolls slagging off Eurosport for pulling a live stage. It was too complicated to explain. We moved on.

'SAY WHAT YOU LIKE ABOUT THE SWISS, BUT THE FLAG'S A BIG PLUS.'

Matera in southern Italy is an amazing place. It was settled in ancient times by troglodytes; that's 'cave dwellers' to you and me. It's been around for thousands of years and some of the caves higher up the hill above the town are just as they were in the time of Christ. Mel Gibson filmed *The Passion of the Christ* in this very place. No set required.

These days, many of the caves are fronted by chi-chi restaurant facades and, once shown to your table, you stare about in wonder at the solid rock from which the place was originally carved. The night before the stage, we were installed in one such establishment. A mix of the modern and ancient. 'Imagine how tough life must've been,' I exclaimed, tucking into a plate of lobster claw pasta and an impeccable Pinot Grigio. Irked, Dan flicked a bit of my flying food off his phone, ordered another large beer, and carried on Tweeting.

A place for the Trogs, then. And on this day at Giro 2013 it wasn't just John Degenkolb who was a wild thing. The weather was too.

It all started off nicely enough. The finish line was on a steep uphill ramp into the new town area of Matera, over the hill and out of sight of Mel Gibson's camera angles. We sat at the top of the incline, our commentary position having been levelled with jacks and wooden blocks. It jutted out at an angle to the slope, making the climbing finish feel very real indeed.

We began our commentary in full sunshine, but the pictures from out on course were very different. Bradley Wiggins, riding the Giro after coming out of the winter in poor shape for a Tour defence, crashed in the wet. He wasn't alone.

Slowly the sky darkened, the clouds looking as black as in the tropics. And then the sky burst. The rain fell like a sky ocean had simply flipped over. It was solid. You couldn't see a metre in front. Our position was at the top of a slope with a gradient of perhaps 20%, there was no ground higher than us to funnel the rain. Even so, we were surrounded by sheets of water, rushing away downhill and replenished from the sky. It was mayhem.

The crowds' screams disappeared as they took cover and our screens flickered. We carried on.

No pictures of the finish area could be shown at that moment because the cameras had not been protected from the rain and had to be switched off. We still had race pictures of the riders who, bizarrely, were still in sunshine. They were about to face something that until now only Noah had witnessed. We gamely soldiered on, until – *cruuunk!* The commentary position lurched over at an angle. One of the jacks had been washed away, along with its wooden foot. We were balancing at an angle.

'Tirati fuori da lì!' bellowed the director, and then in English: 'Everybody out!'

First away were the French from beIN SPORTS. Gone in a flash. Poufff! Amazing!

Frankie and Davide from Rai Uno were a little more relaxed, packing up their stuff and ambling out grumbling.

But Dan and I went into captain of the *Titanic* mode and stayed planted. The Brits were going to keep the world feed going, even if we went down with this baby. We carried on. After about 15 minutes, the rain stopped and the sun came out again. Miraculous. Back in came the Italians, soaked to the skin but grinning and saluting us with winks and slaps on the back. We were being jiggled back level as the jacks were reinstated on fresh blocks.

I don't remember the French coming back. Their production had ended with the commentators' 'escape'.

For the record, John Degenkolb came up the hill to win. The changing tent had been washed away in the tempest, so he was guided to the rear of the podium by Valentina to await the call to the stage. Some fresh kit arrived and, without a thought, he stripped off completely to change. Valentina came into the commentary position in a state of shock.

'You OK, Valentina? You look terrified. Did you have a bad time out there?' I enquired.

'No. It's not the weather. And it is not a bad thing that I have seen. But yes, I am in shock. . .'

'Why, what's happened to you?'

'I say this only to you. John Degenkolb. He is in my top . . . er . . . one!'

THOSE CALF MUSCLES! I THINK HE'S SMUGGLING FROZEN CHICKENS!

'And now we return to our live transmission with announcers Carol-Tone Kurby and Daniel Lloyd. And I can tell you that the contestants are just heading for a big action point of the day . . .'

This was a genuine throw to us from Steve, the continuity guy, on an American cable network as they returned from an ad break. I am not joking.

OK, this 'announcer' hasn't heard riders called 'contestants' before or since, but it was indicative of how cycling is viewed stateside. It ain't big bananas. Our American cousins are too infatuated with baseball, basketball and their version of football.

They don't really get cycling. Despite the fact that there are more cyclists in the US than just about anywhere, it's not box office and it rates poorly.

They can't get their head round the idea that the overall winner of a race may not have even won a stage himself. I do have a bit of sympathy with this view. Anyway, when it comes to paying for the broadcasting rights of races like the Tour of California, Utah, or the now defunct US Pro Challenge in Colorado, the production gig usually goes out to tender. And the winner, who gets to bring the race to an international audience, has, in the past, been the lowest bidder. It's a cost thing.

Cycling is not cheap and globally often has government backing. Not in the USA. This means they don't have enough helicopters, relay equipment or production skills and as a result the races are always losing pictures. On the US Pro Challenge we lost pictures so frequently that broadcasters pulled from the event. It died in 2015. I'm not surprised.

In 2011, George Hincapie was the hero of the race launched by Lance Armstrong the year before. Although George was a doper he was a fully 'fessed-up doper, which, in the strange world of cycling, makes the fact he cheated kind of alright – with some at least. His misdemeanours were ignored in the daily stage reports. Incidentally, the only way to cure a varicose vein is to pull the whole thing out and he wanted to keep the blood supply there. So he and the bunch of grapes on his left calf rode on together. Fair enough.

Hincapie is an all-American, square-jawed jock. On Stage 2 of the 2011 race, he was a striking physical presence as he pushed on towards Aspen. He flew down off a big escarpment heading into town, leading the race in an epic battle against several riders, including his compadres Tejay van Garderen and Tom Danielson along with two Colombians. Then – nothing. The pictures stopped and the director cut away to, you guessed it, the finish line and shots of spectators drinking microbrewery beer. We had the usual loop of images, this time about 15 minutes long. That is a long run of airtime without any action.

My director at Eurosport told me, 'Sorry, commentators, we have nothing to replace this programme – you have to keep going.'

It's at moments like this I actually thrive, partly because I find it amusing rather than stressful. Other commentators find it terrifying, but I'm happy to engage with whatever pictures I have to work with and talk about, in this case, microbreweries and hot dogs, for an hour or so if necessary. I have no fear of it because I feel the audience is with you at moments like this. And like a comedian on stage, confidence is king . . . so on we ploughed with a few gags here and a Twitter chat there as sketchy reports popped up on the web from the team cars themselves. Essentially we had nothing. So I began to create scenarios of what might be happening. The audience lapped it up. To avoid boredom, I started referring to George Hincapie as Gorgeous George, the name of a famous post-war American wrestler. I was busy shooting the breeze when *bam!* the pictures were back and George Hincapie emerged from the trees leading a five-up sprint. We snapped back into action with my previous comments locked in place: ' . . . and here comes Gorgeous George.'

And so it went on to the line. George won.

You'd think the American fans watching on hooky feeds might have appreciated my perhaps over-familiar tones towards one of their sons. Oooooh no! Twitter lit up:

'Stop all this gay talk.'

'Gay is not the way!'

'Take your gayness way back to Europe, man!'

Yep, we lost a few that day. No harm done.

'HE LIKES A BOILED EGG... ACTUALLY, I JUST MADE THAT UP.'

COMPLAINTS DEPARTMENT

Like many pro riders, Dan Lloyd never really had a proper job until he stopped riding. By then he was 29. Since then, he's got very grown-up and a bit more sensible. A bit. As with all riders, the clock stopped on his maturing self as soon as he signed up to ride professionally – at an age when he was still pretty juvenile. Cycling teams are full of teenage-style mischief. And the joy of this can prove addictive, drifting into the world of grown-ups later.

Every day during a long tour, the French commentators from beIN were banging on about how one particular sheet of information was being displayed. This useful page, the GC Par Dossard, is quite simply the entire field noted in numerical team order, with each rider's time delay on the leader listed next to his name. It is a very useful tool in commentary because you can immediately see if, for example, a group of breakaway riders is a threat to the race leader. It is also a great reference when any rider pops up on screen from within the pack, giving you a steer as to whether or not his race is going well. The beef from our French friends was that for the first 10 days of the race this sheet of paper also had a thin black line drawn through the names of those riders who were out of the event. Now, though, this thin line was missing as a visual aid. Instead of a name crossed through, what you saw was a blank time next to the name. The press information officer clearly thought that was enough, but the French wanted their black lines back. They were very uppity about it.

There are so many things to get agitated about in working on the road and this was not one of them. Dan was getting annoyed. 'What's their problem, FFS? Why don't they just draw on the black lines through the names themselves?'

On and on the French ranted each day as they checked the information document to see if the black lines had been reinstated. A flamboyant 'Boufff!!!' meant they had not.

About two weeks in, I found Dan early to the comms box, quietly working.

'You alright?' I ventured. I'd not seen such dedication before.

'Yep… all good.' He beavered on.

I looked over his shoulder. 'Oh, you filling in the black lines for the Chuckle Brothers, are you?'

'Kind of,' said Dan with his trademark staccato 'Ha-ha-ha-ha' (always bursts of four for some reason).

Dan had very carefully filled in the black lines over the names of those out of the race. *But* he had also drawn a line through the main French guy in the race, Pierre Rolland.

'You swine,' I said, smiling.

Dan was dedicated to his craft. He had to do this twice because both the lead commentator and his co-commentator would have their own. It took Dan ages.

In came the French and began to change as they would soon be presenting their pre-show, VVV: Very Very Vélo… or something equally badly named that they were proud of.

And right on cue, Alex picks up the dossier and flicks straight to GC Par Dossard. 'Aaaaaah, at laaast!' he shouted over to Dan. 'They have done it! Good.'

Dan smiled and said nothing.

Off went the French to their outside pre-show live position in front of us.

'This'll be good,' said Dan excitedly.

'You've got to tell them, Dan. They'll see it live on air and think Rolland is out. They'll go nuts about it. He's their big name.'

Just then, we were counted in for our own, out of vision pre-show. There was no time to tell our French friends about the landmine that had been planted in their notes.

A man in meltdown is not a pretty sight. But it is a funny one. Sadly, our own broadcast was also affected. As we tried to work, we saw, out of the corner of our eyes, our impeccably dressed French friends slamming down the paper on to their wobbly mock desk in a field. We soldiered on. About 10 minutes later, the French stormed the commentary position. 'Who has done this!? Whooooo!????'

We shrugged.

'SHEEP DROPPINGS MAKE AMAZING HAND GRENADES.'

24
HOW DO YOU FEEL?

'Mate, I'm . . . I'm knackered. . . Just . . . piss off . . . for a bit . . . will you?'

Bradley Wiggins keeping it real after his fantastic time trial at the 2012 Dauphiné.

Anyone would have sympathy with the panting, tortured, exhausted athlete in a situation like this. 'Give the guy some space!' you shout at the TV. But just as the Directeur Sportif has been screaming radio instructions to get the best out of the rider, so too do TV producers now spank the ears of the poor reporters: 'Get to the front of that mosh-pit FFS. We need Wiggins *nowww!*'

Getting a good interview from a rider after he's just completed a gruelling time trial, or spent four hours hacking up a series of mountains, is not easy. It takes a bit of finessing – not easy in a competitive environment. The finish line reporter has rivals in the hunt for the first reaction. Getting a handle on those around you as well as the target interviewee is difficult.

The reporters gather by the rider like a group of hyenas holding back from taking the first bite out of an exhausted wildebeest – partly because the first one in is likely to get a good kicking.

Everyone knows the rider has just gone to the very limit of his physical, mental and emotional capabilities. To get the best response, many planets must be in line. It helps if:

1. He knows you

2. He likes or respects you

3. It's worth it – i.e. you are from a media company with clout.

None of the above matters a jot if:

1. You are not in the right place

2. You are too pushy

3. You ask a stupid question.

So you get your moment. The rider, still panting, tips his forehead your way while being towelled down and swigging from a bottle. You're on!!! At that moment, all the other schmucks in the press corps are now in your wake. It's your micro-gig. So don't blow it!

Stress hits peak and your eyeballs start to throb a little as your blood pressure rockets. You can hear your own heartbeat echoing in the little cave of your open mouth. Your mind stalls, time for a lifebelt. *Here it comes! Oh no, not that stupid line. There must be another one in there somewhere?! . . . Nope. Nothing.* So you go with the laziest, most banal, unresearched bollocks question from page one of *Dumb Reporting for Dummies*: 'How do you feel?'

Before the rider answers into the jostling multicoloured microphones, there's a muffled chorus of 'Oh, FFS . . .' from all the other reporters who have made the scene.

If it's Mark Cavendish in front of you, and he's in the mood for mischief, you get the bullet: 'Using me hands. Next question.' He points at another more capable reporter and you're done.

'How do you feel?' is a question excusable only for those for whom English is not a first language. For the rest, this is a question that falls from the mouths of only those at the lame end of the broadcast journo spectrum. Yes, it may well be an open-ended question that can't be answered with a simple 'yes' or 'no'. But asking it means you'll be found out as either green or lazy. It's too common. Pack it in.

WIN, AND YOU TALK. LOSE, AND YOU WALK

Some riders really resent the media and PR part of their job. It is an inconvenient by-product of success. As a stage winner, or race leader, there is a press conference to attend. Everyone else can go.

Cycling is not a stadium event, so there is usually a journey to be getting on with at the end of a long day's racing in order to get into position for the following stage in the morning. This inevitably means that time spent talking with the press is a nibble at the precious rest and preparation schedule of the big name cyclist.

Yes, you can remind riders – and their own team manager will do – that public relations is indeed part of a tidy contract that brings them, if they are good, great rewards. Cycling is a sport that relies almost entirely on private sponsorship. And the sugar daddy team owners and race organisers need to see the stars wearing their kit and talking nicely about their day. It's a brand management thing. And to keep the wheels from coming off the bandwagon, the stars are expected to play along.

So sorry, superstar, the contract clearly states: 'You must suck it up and engage with the press and public . . . even when you are physically and mentally shot to bits.' (Obviously, they put this in lawyer speak.)

What the contract does not say, however, is that they have to like it. And often they don't. This can make for a stressful time in front of mikes and cameras. The way this is handled often reflects on the personality of the rider – or 'victim', as they sometimes see themselves.

THE TOUGH GUY

Mark Cavendish's twitching jaw muscle has become legendary in the world of cycling journalism. Once that starts to go, you know you're in for a rough ride.

Meet Tim: BBC trainee. Nervous, overawed and underqualified. He's been parachuted in to have a go at a sport that is frankly way down the pecking order at the Beeb, what with the distractions of Wimbledon and *Match of the Day*.

Tim has all the badges. Tim, therefore, has all the access. Tim is now standing in front of a man who has sized Tim up. Cav is ready. Tim is not. Let battle commence:

Tim: 'Hi! I'm Tim.'

Cav: *Silence. Jaw twitching. Eyes narrow.*

Tim [*perspiring*]: 'Right, let's start off with today, shall we?'

Cav: 'No, let's end with today. One question!'

Tim: 'Your people said five minutes.'

Cav: 'One question. Or none, if you like. There's a queue behind you.'

Tim has now dropped his notes: 'Er . . . how do you feel?'

Cav: 'Alright, thanks for askin'. See ya.'

Cav is now addressing Daniel Friebe's microphone. Daniel is a known and trusted ITV reporter who immediately settles the nerves with a well-judged, insightful question. Meanwhile, Tim is busy pushing through the crowd with apparently very little blood left in his face.

Later, at the bar, he's talking to BBC's cycling lead Simon Brotherton, a kindly man. Simon has the look of a counsellor about him. Tim is venting, in spitting whispers, at the sheer injustice of it all: 'Frankly, I find Mister Cavendish simply impenetrable.'

'Here's to Cav' was the giggling toast at the Eurosport table.

THE PSYCHIATRIST

Chris Froome has a reputation for being, well, a bit bland. He is most certainly not. Behind the choirboy facade is a man very capable of saying boo to a goose – or indeed *bollocks* to a journalist, albeit in an oblique manner that you may not fully comprehend until long after you have left the scene. Hours later and well into a couple of pints of wine, journalists have been known to suddenly emerge from deep thought: 'Hang on a mo!!! I think I've been insulted!' Chris Froome is the thinking assassin's assassin. Beware.

Everyone should realise that Froome-Dog, as he is known, is not a pack animal. He hunts alone. He even hunts his friends. Richie Porte was a roommate and best friend of Froomie for years. Chris was helped to much glory by his Aussie pal. Then Richie departed for BMC for the chance to spread his own wings. When Richie was on the cusp of winning the Dauphiné of 2017, Froome-Dog went rabid on his mate's ass. He organised a cross-team bully squad to attack his former teammate and later speared through a corner on a challenging descent in a move of such audacity that the commissaires initially thought they couldn't sanction it because it was so brutally brilliant in terms of TV drama. Richie lost the race that he'd led by over a minute. So shaken was he by the move that a few weeks later, when the very same corner was repeated at the Tour de France, he was so busy guarding the 'Froome line' at the apex that he crashed out, breaking his pelvis. Had Froome 'allowed' Richie a clear run at the Dauphiné, many suspect that Porte could have been Tour Champion as well. Mates, eh!?

So if Froome is like that with his pals, don't expect it to be any different when he makes a move towards your microphone.

My dad, Bill, wore the crossed-rifles badge during his tour of duty in the Korean War. He was a mortar bomber but, because of his remarkable marksmanship, was also a defensive sniper, protecting his unit from pesky enemy snipers. Once, over a few pints of bitter, my dad talked about breathing, thought control and the lowering of the heart rate before delivery. To kill, you must be calm. This is also the best tool in the psychiatrist's locker: To open up the unwary, the good doctor needs to create an air of total and utter calm. The patient's defences are thus reduced. He feels safe on the couch as the mind investigator begins his work.

Here comes Dr Christopher Froome FRCPsych, who now addresses the patient. Sorry, journalist.

Chris reveals a row of pearly baby teeth as he takes his seat. He begins the conversation with a Zen starter: 'And how are you today?'

Korean Radio reporter: 'Oh, very well, thank you. Why are you so much better than anyone else in cycling?'

Now this question comes from a country without a solid heritage in cycling. As a sport, road cycling in Korea sits some way below eSports arena computer gaming in terms of TV ratings. So the question is from a reporter who's rather out of his depth but trying to be polite.

Somebody at his journalism college must have told him to keep nodding and smiling. He looks like the waving, happy cat you see at the till in sushi bars, but it's his head that's moving at fixed tempo, not his arm. He looks happy enough, but he's terrified.

Dr Chris [*looking deep into his soul, and smiling gently*]: 'It's very kind of you to say, but I don't really know where to begin on that one, so I'll tell you about why I'm here today, shall I? Goooood.'

Chris is now in total control. He goes on to talk through precisely what he wants to. He manages this in a flawlessly professional and considered way. I've seen well-informed old hacks tooled up with killer questions who simply melt under this onslaught of calm.

Even in the dark days, when many in the press corps were convinced he had broken rules on the meds permitted for his asthma, this man remained a beacon of calm and decorum in hostile press conferences. Froome controls the flow. And makes you go with it too. Genius.

THE BEST MATE

The Eurosport anchor Jonathan Edwards is already smiling. He knows what's next. G is dropping in. Happy days. Anchoring on live TV can be a juggling act. Some guests are difficult. Sometimes you have to work hard to open up an oyster. And then there is Geraint Thomas . . .

Jonathan's cheeks are now hurting, his smile muscles slowly setting to stone: 'Welcome Geraint Thomas, who today has taken over the yellow jersey.'

In slides our pal, still panting after a short jog from another broadcaster. Minders everywhere, but our star remains unflummoxed. While being miked up, he opens in trademark unabashed style:

'Wow. Knackered. Really knackered. Sorry, tired. It's been quite a day.'

Jonathan: 'Tell us about it.'

G: 'Well . . .'

Aaaaaand he's off!!!! Full gallop.

Out pours a string of funny, well considered, never barbed, cleverly observed one-liners and vignettes of joyfulness. The guy's a star and we all gaze on attentively – not with a sense of subservient reverence, but because we know he'll have a story to tell that's well worth a few minutes of our time. When G is on TV, the world melts away for the viewer. It's just like listening to a tale from a mate down the pub. He can describe a stage of professional cycling in great detail yet with a simple sense of wonder and humour wrapped up with a healthy dose of self-deprecation. The audience is chomping at the bit. It's like listening to your drinking pal who's just shared a tube ride with Kate Moss. 'Give us the detail!!!' you beg. And he does. Top bloke.

THE OPTIMIST

For the uninitiated, you could come across Esteban Chaves for the first time and wonder if he was alright in the head. He never stops smiling! Now, I smile a lot. I'm amused by life. Chaves, however, is amused by life, strife and everything else. Whatever he's having for breakfast, I want.

Considering what Esteban has gone through in his career, it's remarkable he's been able to remain so chipper. A horror crash in 2013 at Trofeo Laigueglia left him with a fractured everything. Many thought he would never make it back to the top. Well, he did. And part of that remarkable recovery was his overwhelming sense of fun and wonder. It's infectious.

Unimaginative reporter: 'How do you feel?'

Esteban [with trademark grin]: 'Yeah, it's great! I'm good! Goood!'

Reporter: 'But you lost the stage. What about your rivals, Esteban, they really stuck it into you today?'

Esteban looks down for a moment but never stops smiling. Softly he says: 'Sure, it hurts to lose...' Then bouncing back into the zone: 'But hey! We are all friends, no?!'

I love Esteban.

THE ENIGMA

Nairo Quintana stunned everyone in 2014 with some gutsy, aggressive rides that brought him his first Grand Tour. Two years after the pink jersey at Giro d'Italia, he took the red one at La Vuelta. Since then, Nairo has kind of retreated from the battlefront. He has become an extremely cautious rider. Seemingly, he follows rather than leads attacks and the results on the big tours have dried up. It's as if his ambitions are getting locked down. He's much the same in interviews.

The temptation for any interviewer must be to wave a hand in front of Quintana's blankly staring face in a kind of *hello?!* moment, just to check for consciousness. And it's not just with reporters. Apparently he is likewise disengaged even within his own team. In the past, he has been reminded by his manager that it might be a good idea to go back down the bus and thank his teammates who have just worked themselves ragged and delivered him to a stage win. It's not something he is naturally given to doing. It's not nastiness. He is just not a communicator. At all.

Despite his career success and notoriety, Quintana is an easy man to walk by away from the race. He is remarkably anonymous. You just don't notice him.

Nairo is a bit of an enigma, wrapped up in a conundrum. He can't be reached. You can try – and people do. But nobody has made contact. Not really.

Juan Antonio Flecha, jolly as you like, lovely guy, former rider. A no-pressure interviewer because he doesn't need to be. He gets a lot from riders, as he is well respected and super-well-informed: 'Hey, Nairo, what a day with so many changes out there. What was the battle plan?'

Nairo: 'Er . . .'

Flecha: 'Was it to send satellite riders up the mountain to bridge to?'

Nairo: 'Yes. . . it was.'

Flecha [*smile fixing with anxiety*]: 'Well, it seemed to be going well until that penultimate test!?'

Nairo: 'We work hard.'

Flecha [*heading into begging mode*]: 'So where did it go wrong, Nairo?'

Nairo: 'My legs, not good.'

Flecha [*abandoning while filling in the gaps*]: 'Thank you, Nairo. Good luck for tomorrow. Let's hope with two days of hard climbing to go, the strategy comes good for you guys. All the best.'

Nairo: 'Yes.'

Nairo remains seated, staring into space, waiting for a crew member to collect him.

THE JOKER

Peter Sagan is a man who has defined an era. His freewheeling style is a joy to behold, except if he's shoulder-charging you in a sprint. He is the definition of freestyle cycling. He rides like nobody else. When the fashion was for long lead-out trains, Sagan went the other way. With so many trains at the station, he simply hopped, hobo style, on to other people's carriages. Long lines of riders, each in team order, would approach high-speed finales as well-drilled units. Meanwhile, Sagan merrily hopped from one to another, barging his way in. He got a free ride from the best. His teammates were used up far earlier in a stage. They set the approach pace with about 20km (12 miles) to go. One by one, they burned themselves out as other teams began to panic. Riders were strewn everywhere as teams tried to hold it together as a unit. Sagan stayed mostly solo and solid, part of a team but the ultimate individual. He would choose his time and charge on alone. Sagan might go early, might go late, but nobody knew when. That was for Sagan to decide. It's brought him three World Championship titles and effectively killed off long lead outs. They're much shorter these days. Two in front of the sprinter is now a maximum inside the flamme rouge. Sagan showed the way on this. Being flexible and wheel-hopping is difficult if you are working a line dance. Sagan might use one lead-out man before going it alone far earlier than most.

Sagan is his own man. Which makes him a devil to deal with in an interview. He plays reporters like a kid boxer. He knows he can knock them out at any time. They can pretend to spar with him, but this just makes him laugh. Get serious, and he goes the other way. Get funny, and it's over. He is a tough nut to crack.

Ashley House, the Eurosport anchor who loves his cycling, and is an engaging, enthusiastic good guy: 'Peter, great to see you out there and so dominant in the end!?'

Sagan [voice like a hornet trapped in a jam jar]: 'Well, you know how it is. Bah! Life . . . what can I say?'

Ashley: 'Well, talk us through those last 500 metres.'

Sagan [smirking as if trying to hold in a giggle]: 'Well, some go left, some go right. I go straight. I win. What can I say?'

Ashley: 'Well, hopefully a bit more! [*Nervous chuckle.*] You look solid in green, Peter. Is this your target now, to stay safe, or can we expect more from you over the next few difficult days?'

Sagan [clearly impatient]: 'Ah, we will see.'

Ashley [with one last attempt]: 'Tell us about those ski goggles you have around your neck? It's 35 degrees!'

Sagan, who is blatantly wearing a sponsor's kit from another sport entirely: 'I like them a lot. . . Bye!'

And with that he's gone stage right towards another poor soul who will try and dig deeper. No chance.

THE ZEN MONK

He's called Cadel Evans but some of us wonder if his real name is Kunchen Evans – this being a Tibetan name that translates as 'All-Knowing'. Cadel knows what he likes. And he doesn't like talking much. This is not because he doesn't want to engage, it is simply that his mind is so powerful it kind of gets in the way a bit. Cadel is a thinker extraordinaire. Ask him a question, and the silence will be broken only by a faint tinkling of bells coming from his ears as he goes deep to find meaning in the words you have uttered. He will answer, but this may take time. Many things must be considered before Kunchen speaks.

It's 1998 and Cadel Evans is doing great things as a youngster at the Tour VTT Mountain Bike Tour de France. I am the reporter. A bit of polite banter before we even begin: 'Hi, Cadel, how are you today?' Silence.

Uh oh, he's off already. Cadel begins to stare. He looks past my left ear into the distance. I've lost him; Cadel has gone deep. The question bounces around his massive brain like a bee in the dome of St Paul's Cathedral. After a while, his lips begin to move well before any sound comes out. His voice, when it does come, is like a children's entertainer very slowly explaining how the universe was formed. It's as if he's seeking the answer himself while responding. He repeats the question back at me: 'How . . . am I . . . today?' and then silence again. But at least the eyes are back in the house. His body is still, but his brain remains busy; just coming down off overload. He's still thinking to himself: *Wow, today . . . how are things? As opposed to yesterday? Or what they may be tomorrow? Hmmm, this is a toughie.*

Me: 'Cadel? You ok?'

Cadel [*very slowly*]: 'Sure. Er, things are good. . . Really good. . . Thanks . . . for asking.'

And so begins a series of questions that take for ever to get a response. When each answer does come, despite great thought and contemplation, they are short and un-complex.

So a sequence of inviting questions from me come back with: 'Good.' 'Fine, yeah.' 'Tough, yes.' It's as if he thinks I would be entirely incapable of coping with the real answer he has been contemplating during the *long* pauses. These far deeper answers have now been locked away in a cerebral golden casket to be retrieved later. Much later, when the Sun implodes. It's not good TV.

Of course, Cadel's legs responded far faster than his tongue. Lucky for him. Not for me. Cadel went on to become a Tour de France winner and World Champion. I watched him thrive with great fondness. He was and indeed remains among my favourite riders of all time.

His interview skills did get better. A little.

But I still hear bells when I think of him.

'HE'S A BIT OF A SWISS ARMY KNIFE RIDER – HE CAN DO ANYTHING.'

25
THE PARTY'S OVER

29 July 2018

I stand at the end of the Champs Elysées after the awards ceremony and idly kick a bit of yellow confetti off my shoe. It's another British winner of the Tour de France, the sixth one in eight years. Incredible to think that before 2012 no Brit had ever won.

I feel a sense of great pride – and relief. This, mixed with a combination of a mild patriotic tingling and extreme exhaustion, makes me well up with emotion. I'm given to that even on air, as you know. But I don't have to choke it back this time and my eyes duly fill up with tears. I blink them away and turn towards the Place de la Concorde, not far from the finish. I take a left up to Place de la Madeleine. This square is off-course and the taxi rank near the boutique for Maille mustard is usually accommodating. Apologising softly, in that very English way, I bump past revelling spectators in the street. My job on this Tour is done.

It'll be a quiet night on my own. I'm too spent to join the rest of the TV crowd for the wrap party. I just want to be somewhere really quiet and not speak another word. I feel like the time triallist who gives his absolute all, right up until the finish line, whereupon he collapses into an exhausted heap. I've given it everything too, and now it's all over I can barely mutter a word.

For those who have been locked in a production truck, this is party time! For me, I've been the party host on every single stage. I have been 'up and on it' for three weeks. Most of my colleagues have been quiet and focused for the same period. So the graphics guys, editors, producers, directors, play-in staff, and so on now have a chance to let their hair down. I have very little hair. And what I have left will not be going anywhere near a nightclub.

I always take a quiet modest hotel next to the Gare du Nord, where I go deep into monk mode, as I call it. I buy a Chinese takeaway – as un-French a meal as possible. After 21 stages, I've usually had my fill of the local stuff. Maybe I'll have a beer, but Belgian or German only.

I hole up in my room. No company, no TV, no bright light. Quiet.

I just sit there on my own, eating as slowly as I can – unlike the refuelling feeding style I've endured for too long at work. As I dine, I reflect on the past three weeks of excitement, fun, boredom, exhaustion, good and bad meals, nights in stuffy rooms, nights in luxurious rooms, thousands of kilometres of tarmac covered in a hire car, the camaraderie and enmity of colleagues, the incredible feats of heroism and brilliance from the riders and, of course, the thought that another British rider has added to the chagrin of the keepers of cycling's Holy Grail – the French, Belgians, Italians and Spaniards. I smile. I am at peace. I am alone.

Tomorrow I have a first-class ticket on an old-fashioned train with super-comfy seats that will whisk me to Rue station near the Picardy coast. My lovely wife, Steph, and our adorable kids, Margot and Teddy, will meet me there and whisk me off to paradise: Les Tourelles is a chateau hotel full of old-world charm right on the beach at Le Crotoy, a humble fishing village at the mouth of the Somme estuary. It has a harbour dotted with a few modest restaurants and a tidal beach with sand as soft as milled white pepper. Room 14 overlooks the sea, facing south-west. I can sit by the open French windows and the little balconette to breathe in the fresh air and drink in the beautiful view, along with a glass of Jupiler draft beer from the lovely bar downstairs. Here I can come down as easy as a seagull gliding off a cliff. Silence. Well, for about half an hour. 'Come on, Dad!' Forget cycling. It's now time to wrestle. I've missed my gang!

26
AND SO IT COMES TO THIS

Cycling, at its heart, is an individual sport. On the bike, you are largely on your own out there. If you are doing it properly, there is not much chit-chat. Sure, you are part of a team and once you've got your breath back, it's great to gather together at a pub or café and recount what you've just conquered, whether that be Winnats Pass or the Staines bypass. Cycling, then, is a gang of individuals. TV sports broadcasting is much the same.

As a commentator, you are pretty much on your own. Yes, I have a sherpa next to me on the ascent, but when it comes to the words that I use, I am alone on stage; naked except for the red Vuelta roadbook in front of my bits as everyone points and laughs. Sorry, that last bit was a recent nightmare.

Anyway, back to the point: I am the last man standing in the process of the production. My words, once spoken, cannot be retrieved. They will hit the Moon after around 18 minutes and then drift off into the universe. They are, indeed, all said and done. I don't have auto-correct, except if Kelly starts star-jumping and mouthing, 'Noooooooooo!' It is my responsibility to put the cherry on top of the broadcast cake. Some agree that what I do is indeed the final touch; they just reckon it's more akin to bird poo on the roof of a Ferrari.

There is a pyramid of staff that bring cycling to your screens. The race organisers and all their infighting and funding issues. The local councils and police, national sports bodies and sanctioning authorities. The rights negotiation crew and the booking staff. Operations managers and logistics. Helicopters, motorcycles, cars and trucks. Barriers, catering and cables. Data, rigging, power, guidebooks – and much more. Every job that has to be done has a team that got every single person or thing into position. Even just the TV bit: cars, tickets, passes, hotels, cameras, graphics, planners, producers, directors, lighting, sound, make-up – and those are just some of the items on what is a very long list.

Fast-forward to the action that actually pops up on your screen. If *everything* comes together in this mega-operation, then all you have to do is press a few keys or buttons and have your favourite sport, in all its magnificence, set before you.

And then I go and tell you what I think about it. This will either go down well or it will go down badly.

What I do for a living is a privilege. I love cycling and I love my job. It's a hell of a merry-go-round. For now, yippee! I still have a book of tickets. One day, inevitably, I will take my last ride. In the meantime, I'm going to carry on having fun and wholeheartedly invite you all to join me.

So until the spinning stops, I say –

To my fans: 'Hi gang!'

To those who put up with me: 'Thank you.'

And to those who really don't like me much: 'Sorry.'

Bye for now.

Carlton Kirby

ABOUT THE AUTHORS

Carlton Kirby is the principal cycling commentator for Eurosport and has covered the Tour de France, the Giro d'Italia and Vuelta a España among many other cycling races.

He has worked in broadcasting for over thirty years, over which time he has accumulated legions of loyal fans who are drawn to his witty and, at times, excitable style. Known by some as the 'language mangler' and for his 'Kirbyisms' (occasional strange musings about not just cycling but the very fabric of life), loyal listeners have set up a Twitter account of his humorous comments: Things Carlton Says, @saidcarlton.

Robbie Broughton is the co-founder and managing editor of *Ride Velo*, an online magazine that covers features, profiles, product reviews and news of the professional cycling world.

Living in a traditional Mallorcan village he likes nothing more than setting off on his bike into the Tramuntana mountains in a deluded attempt to emulate his cycling heroes.

ACKNOWLEDGEMENTS

Well it took some time coming, but finally a window into my world is here. Two years ago Robbie Broughton pitched up at Eurosport, my long-suffering and benevolent employers, to interview me for his @ridevelo site. It was supposed to be a 20-minute appointment and we ended up talking for a couple of hours. I don't think Robbie got a word in. Finally he could take no more as his cheeks were aching thanks to his fixed grin. We'd had fun. He asked if I'd ever thought of writing a book. I had of course but this life of mine gets busy. A series of recorded chats were planned and slotted into the season between and during races. Robbie corralled my thoughts and witterings into a series of chapters and I then Kirby-fied what you have in your hands. I have to thank my family for respecting the closed door to my office. I owe Stephanie, Teddy and Margot a fine holiday or two.

Writing can steal a part of one's soul but I've enjoyed the journey. So what you have in your hands is a slice of me gladly given. I hope you enjoy the ride ... that way we can plan another together!

INDEX